STUDY GUIDE AND WORKING PAPERS CHAPTERS 1–12

COLLEGE ACCOUNTING
A Practical Approach
Twelfth Edition

Jeffrey Slater

North Shore Community College
Danvers, Massacusetts

PEARSON

Boston Columbus Indianapolis New York San Francisco Upper Saddle River
Amsterdam Cape Town Dubai London Madrid Milan Munich Paris Montreal Toronto
Delhi Mexico City Sao Paulo Sydney Hong Kong Seoul Singapore Taipei Tokyo

VP/Editorial Director: Sally Yagan
Acquisitions Editor: Lacey Vitetta
Development Editor: Mignon Tucker
Editorial Project Managers: Nicole Sam and Christina Rumbaugh
Editorial Assistants: Jane Avery and Lauren Zanedis
Director of Marketing: Maggie Moylan Leen
Marketing Assistants: Ian Gold and Kimberly Lovato
Senior Managing Editor: Nancy Fenton
Senior Production Project Manager: Roberta Sherman

Manufacturing Buyer: Carol Melville
Cover Designer: Anthony Gemmellaro
Media Project Manager, Production: John Cassar
Media Project Manager: Sarah Peterson
Full-Service Project Management: GEX Publishing Services
Composition: GEX Publishing Services
Printer/Binder: Edwards Brothers Malloy
Cover Printer: Edwards Brothers Malloy
Text Font: Times Roman 10/12

PEARSON

www.pearsonhighered.com

10 9 8 7 6 5 4 3 2
ISBN 10: 0-13-277215-9
ISBN 13: 978-0-13-277215-0

Contents

STUDY GUIDE AND WORKING PAPERS CHAPTERS 1–12

1

INTRODUCTION TO ACCOUNTING CONCEPTS AND PROCEDURES

INSTANT REPLAY: SELF-REVIEW QUIZ 1-1

GRACIE RYAN REAL ESTATE

	ASSETS		=	LIABILITIES	+	OWNER'S EQUITY
	Cash	+	Computer Equipment	=	Accounts Payable	+	Gracie Ryan, Capital
TRANSACTION 1						
NEW BALANCE			=			
TRANSACTION 2						
NEW BALANCE			=			
TRANSACTION 3						
ENDING BALANCE		+		=		+	
				=			

INSTANT REPLAY: SELF-REVIEW QUIZ 1-2

ASSETS							LIABILITIES AND OWNER'S EQUITY						

INSTANT REPLAY: SELF-REVIEW QUIZ 1-3

B. BING CO.

	ASSETS			=	LIABILITIES	+	OWNER'S EQUITY			
	Cash +	Accounts Receivable +	Cleaning Equipment	=	Accounts Payable +		B. Bing, Capital −	B. Bing, Withd. +	Revenue −	Expenses
Beg. Balance	$10,000 +	$2,500 +	$6,500	=	$1,000 +	+	$11,800 −	$800 +	$9,000 −	$2,000
1.				=						
Balance				=						
2.				=						
Balance				=						
3.				=						
Balance				=						
4.				=						
Balance				=						
5.				=						
Ending Balance	+	+		=	+		−	+	−	−

INSTANT REPLAY: SELF-REVIEW QUIZ 1-4

(1)

(2)

(3)

ASSETS				LIABILITIES AND OWNER'S EQUITY				

FORMS FOR DEMONSTRATION PROBLEM

(1)

MICHAEL BROWN, ATTORNEY AT LAW

	ASSETS				= LIABILITIES +				OWNER'S EQUITY					
	Cash	+	Accounts Receivable	+	Office Equipment	=	Accounts Payable	+	M. Brown, Capital	−	M. Brown Withd.	+	Legal fees	− Expenses
A.														
Balance														
B.														
Balance														
C.														
Balance														
D.														
Balance														
E.														
Balance														
F.														
Balance														
G.														
Balance														
H.														
Balance														
I.														
Ending Balance														

FORMS FOR EXERCISES A OR B

1A-1 OR 1B-1

A. _____

B. _____

C. _____

1A-2 OR 1B-2

ASSETS	=	LIABILITIES	+	OWNER'S EQUITY
A.				
B.				
C.				

1A-3 OR 1B-3

RAUSCHER CO.
BALANCE SHEET
APRIL 30, 201X

ASSETS				LIABILITIES AND OWNER'S EQUITY			

EXERCISES (CONTINUED)

1A-4 OR 1B-4

ASSETS			= LIABILITIES	+	OWNER'S EQUITY			
Cash	+ Accounts Receivable	+ Computer Equipment	= Accounts Payable	+	B. Baker Capital	− B. Baker Withd.	+ Revenue	− Expenses
A.								
B								
C.								
D								
E.								
F								
G.								
Ending Balance								

EXERCISES (CONCLUDED)

1A-5 OR 1B-5

(A)

FRECHETTE REALTY
INCOME STATEMENT
FOR MONTH ENDED SEPTEMBER 30, 201X

(B)

FRECHETTE REALTY
STATEMENT OF OWNER'S EQUITY
FOR MONTH ENDED SEPTEMBER 30, 201X

(C)

FRECHETTE REALTY
BALANCE SHEET
SEPTEMBER 30, 201X

ASSETS			LIABILITIES AND OWNER'S EQUITY		

END OF CHAPTER PROBLEMS

PROBLEM 1A-1 OR PROBLEM 1B-1

MIKE'S NAIL SPA

	ASSETS		=	LIABILITIES	+	OWNER'S EQUITY
	Cash	+	Store Equipment	=	Accounts Payable	+	Mike, Ackerman, Capital
TRANSACTION A						
NEW BALANCE						
TRANSACTION B						
NEW BALANCE						
TRANSACTION C						
NEW BALANCE						
TRANSACTION D						
ENDING BALANCE						

PROBLEM 1A-2 OR PROBLEM 1B-2

SHIRE'S INTERNET SERVICE
BALANCE SHEET
SEPTEMBER 30, 201X

ASSETS	LIABILITIES AND OWNER'S EQUITY

PROBLEM 1A-5 OR PROBLEM 1B-5 (CONTINUED)

(B)

TRICKETT'S CATERING SERVICE
BALANCE SHEET
MARCH 31, 201X

ASSETS				LIABILITIES AND OWNER'S EQUITY				

(C)

TRICKETT'S CATERING SERVICE
INCOME STATEMENT
FOR MONTH ENDED APRIL 30, 201X

PROBLEM 1A-5 OR PROBLEM 1B-5 (CONCLUDED)

(D)

TRICKETT'S CATERING SERVICE
STATEMENT OF OWNER'S EQUITY
FOR MONTH ENDED APRIL 30, 201X

(E)

TRICKETT'S CATERING SERVICE
BALANCE SHEET
APRIL 30, 201X

ASSETS   LIABILITIES AND OWNER'S EQUITY

CHAPTER 1
SUMMARY PRACTICE TEST:
INTRODUCTION TO ACCOUNTING CONCEPTS AND PROCEDURES

Part I Instructions

Fill in the blank(s) to complete the statement.

1. _____ was passed to prevent corporate fraud.

2. _____ – Liabilities = Owner's Equity

3. The owner's current investment or equity in the assets of a business is called _____.

4. A list of assets, liabilities, and owner's equity as of a particular date is reported on a(n) _____ _____.

5. _____ create an outward or potential outward flow of assets.

6. Revenue earned not on account creates an asset entitled _____.

7. _____ record personal expenses that are not related to the business. They are a subdivision of owner's equity.

8. The _____ _____ reports how well a business performs for a period of time.

9. The _____ _____ _____ _____ is a report that shows changes in capital.

10. The ending figure for capital from the statement of owner's equity is placed on the _____ _____.

Part II Instructions

Answer true or false to the following statements.

1. Accounts Receivable is a liability.
2. Liabilities produce revenue.
3. Revenue is an asset.
4. Capital means cash.
5. Bookkeeping is 50% of accounting.
6. The balance sheet lists assets, revenue, and owner's equity.
7. The balance sheet shows where we are now for a specific period of time.
8. Revenue creates an outward flow of assets.
9. Expenses are a subdivision of owner's equity.
10. Withdrawals are the only subdivision of owner's equity.
11. Withdrawals are listed on the income statement.
12. Revenue is a subdivision of owner's equity.
13. Revenues and withdrawals are listed on the income statement.
14. The income statement helps update the statement of owner's equity, and the statement of owner's equity helps update the balance sheet.
15. Withdrawals are listed on the statement of owner's equity.

Part III Instructions

In column B, record the appropriate code(s) that result from recording the transaction in column A.

1.	Increase in assets	**5.**	Increase in capital
2.	Decrease in assets	**6.**	Increase in revenues
3.	Increase in liabilities	**7.**	Increase in expenses
4.	Decrease in liabilities	**8.**	Increase in withdrawals

COLUMN A	COLUMN B
1. EXAMPLE: Pete Smith invested $5,000 in his business.	1,5
2. Bought computer equipment on account for $600.	_____
3. Paid salaries of $70.	_____
4. Bought additional computer equipment for $750 cash.	_____
5. Paid rent expense of $90.	_____
6. Received $5,000 in cash from revenue earned.	_____
7. Paid heat expense of $15.	_____
8. Earned revenue of $500 that will not be received until next month.	_____
9. Paid amount owed on equipment previously purchased on account.	_____
10. Paid for cleaning supplies expense, $15.	_____
11. Customers paid $10 of amount previously owed.	_____
12. Bought additional equipment of $1,000, half paid in cash and half charged.	_____
13. Charged customer $100 for services performed.	_____
14. Pete paid home phone bill from the company's cash.	_____
15. Advertising expense incurred but not to be paid until next month.	_____

CHAPTER 1 SOLUTIONS TO SUMMARY PRACTICE TEST

Part I

1.	The Sarbanes-Oxley Act	**5.**	Expenses	**9.**	statement of owner's equity
2.	Assets	**6.**	Cash		
3.	capital	**7.**	Withdrawals	**10.**	balance sheet
4.	balance sheet	**8.**	income statement		

Part II

1.	false	**6.**	false	**11.**	false
2.	false	**7.**	false	**12.**	true
3.	false	**8.**	false	**13.**	false
4.	false	**9.**	true	**14.**	true
5.	false	**10.**	false	**15.**	true

Part III

1.	1,5	**6.**	1,6	**11.**	1,2
2.	1,3	**7.**	7,2	**12.**	1,2,3
3.	7,2	**8.**	1,6	**13.**	1,6
4.	1,2	**9.**	4,2	**14.**	8,2
5.	7,2	**10.**	7,2	**15.**	7,3

CONTINUING PROBLEM—ON THE JOB FOR CHAPTER 1

SANCHEZ COMPUTER CENTER

	ASSETS				= LIABILITIES +	OWNER'S EQUITY			
	Cash +	Supplies +	Computer Shop Equipment +	Office Equipment =	Accounts Payable +	Freedman, Capital +	Freedman, – Withdrawals +	Revenue –	Expenses
a									
BALANCE									
b									
BALANCE									
c									
BALANCE									
d									
BALANCE									
e									
BALANCE									
f									
BALANCE									
g									
BALANCE									
h									
BALANCE									
i									
BALANCE									
j									
END BAL.									

SANCHEZ COMPUTER CENTER
INCOME STATEMENT
FOR THE MONTH ENDED JULY 31, 201X

SANCHEZ COMPUTER CENTER
STATEMENT OF OWNER'S EQUITY
FOR MONTH ENDED JULY 31, 201X

SANCHEZ COMPUTER CENTER
BALANCE SHEET
JULY 31, 201X

ASSETS   LIABILITIES AND OWNER'S EQUITY

2

DEBITS AND CREDITS: ANALYZING AND RECORDING BUSINESS TRANSACTIONS

INSTANT REPLAY: SELF-REVIEW QUIZ 2-1

1. _____   4. _____
2. _____   5. _____
3. _____

INSTANT REPLAY: SELF-REVIEW QUIZ 2-2

A.

1. Accounts Affected	2. Category	3. ↑↓	4. Rules	5. T Account Update			

B.

1. Accounts Affected	2. Category	3. ↑↓	4. Rules	5. T Account Update			

C.

1. Accounts Affected	2. Category	3. ↑↓	4. Rules	5. T Account Update				

D.

1. Accounts Affected	2. Category	3. ↑↓	4. Rules	5. T Account Update				

E.

1. Accounts Affected	2. Category	3. ↑↓	4. Rules	5. T Account Update				

INSTANT REPLAY: SELF-REVIEW QUIZ 2-3

Cash	111
4,500	300
2,000	100
1,000	1,200
300	1,300
	2,600

Accounts Payable	211
300	700

Salon Fees	411
	3,500
	1,000

Accounts Receivable	121
1,000	300

Pam Jay, Capital	311
	4,000

Rent Expense	511
1,200	

Salon Equipment	131
700	

Pam Jay, Withdrawals	321
100	

Salon Supplies Exp.	521
1,300	

Salaries Expense	531
2,600	

Name _____ Class _____ Date _____

(1)

_____

_____

_____

(2)

_____

_____

_____

(3)

(4)

DEMONSTRATION PROBLEM (CONTINUED)

(2A)

MICHAEL BROWN, ATTORNEY AT LAW
INCOME STATEMENT
FOR MONTH ENDED JUNE 30, 201X

(2B)

MICHAEL BROWN, ATTORNEY AT LAW
STATEMENT OF OWNER'S EQUITY
FOR MONTH ENDED JUNE 30, 201X

(3C)

MICHAEL BROWN, ATTORNEY AT LAW
BALANCE SHEET
JUNE 30, 201X

| ASSETS | | | | LIABILITIES AND OWNER'S EQUITY | | |

CHAPTER 1
CONCEPT CHECK

1.
  A. _____
  B. _____
  C. _____
  D. _____
  E. _____
  F. _____

2.
  A. _____
  B. _____
  C. _____

3.
  A. _____
  B. _____

4.
  _____
  _____
  _____

5.
  _____
  _____
  _____
  _____
  _____

6.
  _____
  _____
  _____
  _____

7.
  A. _____
  B. _____
  C. _____
  D. _____

8.
  A. _____
  B. _____
  C. _____
  D. _____
  E. _____
  F. _____
  G. _____
  H. _____

9.
  A. _____
  B. _____
  C. _____
  D. _____

PROBLEM 2A-2 OR PROBLEM 2B-2

Cash	111

Brian Pud, Withdrawals	312

Office Equipment	121

Consulting Fees Earned	411

Accounts Payable	211

Advertising Expense	511

Brian Pud, Capital	311

Rent Expense	512

PROBLEM 2A-3 OR PROBLEM 2B-3

(A)

| Cash | 111 | | Accounts Payable | 211 | | Fees Earned | 411 |

| Office Equipment | 121 | | Brad Joy, Capital | 311 | | Rent Expense | 511 |

| | | | Brad Joy, Withdrawals | 312 | | Utilities Expense | 512 |

(B)

BRAD'S CLEANING SERVICE
TRIAL BALANCE
OCTOBER 31, 201X

	Dr.	Cr.

PROBLEM 2A-4 OR PROBLEM 2B-4

(A)

GAIL LUCAS, ATTORNEY AT LAW
INCOME STATEMENT
FOR MONTH ENDED MAY 31, 201X

(B)

GAIL LUCAS, ATTORNEY AT LAW
STATEMENT OF OWNER'S EQUITY
FOR MONTH ENDED MAY 31, 201X

PROBLEM 2A-4 OR PROBLEM 2B-4 (CONCLUDED)

(C)

GAIL LUCAS, ATTORNEY AT LAW
BALANCE SHEET
MAY 31, 201X

ASSETS

LIABILITIES AND OWNER'S EQUITY

PROBLEM 2A-5 OR PROBLEM 2B-5

(1,2,3)

Advertising Expense   511

Gas Expense   512

Salaries Expense   513

Telephone Expense   514

Accounts Payable   211

Avery Annis, Capital   311

Avery Annis, Withdrawals   312

Delivery Fees Earned   411

Cash   111

Accounts Receivable   112

Office Equipment   121

Delivery Trucks   122

PROBLEM 2A-5 OR PROBLEM 2-B5 (CONTINUED)

(4)

ANNIS'S DELIVERY SERVICE
TRIAL BALANCE
AUGUST 31, 201X

		Dr.	Cr.

(5A)

ANNIS'S DELIVERY SERVICE
INCOME STATEMENT
FOR MONTH ENDED AUGUST 31, 201X

PROBLEM 2A-5 OR PROBLEM 2B-5 (CONCLUDED)

(5B)

ANNIS'S DELIVERY SERVICE
STATEMENT OF OWNER'S EQUITY
FOR MONTH ENDED AUGUST 31, 201X

(5C)

ANNIS'S DELIVERY SERVICE
BALANCE SHEET
AUGUST 31, 201X

ASSETS   LIABILITIES AND OWNER'S EQUITY

CHAPTER 2
SUMMARY PRACTICE TEST:
DEBITS AND CREDITS: ANALYZING AND RECORDING
BUSINESS TRANSACTIONS

Part I Instructions

Fill in the blank(s) to complete the statement.

1. Financial reports do not contain _____ or _____.
2. The right side of any T account is called the _____ _____.
3. Assets are increased by _____.
4. The process of balancing an account involves _____.
5. Transaction analysis charts are an aid in recording _____ _____.
6. The _____ _____ _____ indicates the names and numbering system of accounts.
7. A(n) _____ is a group of accounts.
8. A(n) _____ _____ is an informal report that lists accounts and their balances.
9. Withdrawals are increased by _____.
10. The income statement, statement of owner's equity, and balance sheet may be prepared from a(n) _____ _____.
11. Cash, Accounts Receivable, and Equipment are examples of _____.
12. Increasing expenses ultimately cause owner's equity to _____.
13. An increase in rent expense is a(n) _____ by the rules of debits and credits.
14. A debit to one asset and a credit to another asset for the same transaction reflect a(n) _____ in assets.
15. The category of accounts receivable is a(n) _____.

Part II Instructions

Bea Paul opened a shuttle service company. From the following chart of accounts, indicate in column B (by account number) which account (s) will be debited or credited as related to the transaction in column A.

Name _____ Class _____ Date _____

Chart of Accounts

ASSETS	LIABILITIES	EXPENSES
10 Cash	50 Accounts Payable	80 Advertising
20 Accounts Receivable		90 Gas
30 Equipment	OWNER'S EQUITY	100 Salaries
40 Shuttle Bus	60 B. Paul, Capital	110 Telephone
	62 B. Paul, Withdrawals	
	REVENUE	
	70 Taxi Fees Earned	

	COLUMN A	COLUMN B	
		DEBIT(S)	CREDIT(S)
1.	EXAMPLE: Bea Paul invested $40,000 in the shuttle service.	10	60
2.	Purchased a shuttle bus on account for $25,000.		
3.	Bought equipment on account for $3,000.		
4.	Advertising bill received, but not paid until next month, $60.		
5.	Bea paid home telephone bill from company checkbook, $20.		
6.	Collected $100 in cash from daily shuttle fees earned.		
7.	Customer charged a shuttle ride of $20.		
8.	Received partial payment for Transaction #7 of $10.		
9.	Paid business telephone bill, $32.		
10.	Purchased additional equipment for cash, $550.		
11.	Paid shuttle driver salaries of $150.		
12.	Drove customer on account to local train station for $6.		
13.	Received $5 from customer who hired a shuttle for ride across town.		
14.	Collected from past charged revenue, $15.		
15.	Bought office equipment on account for $110.		

Part III Instructions

Answer true or false to the following statements.

1. There are no debit and credit columns found on the three financial statements.
2. A trial balance could balance but be wrong.
3. Withdrawals are listed on the credit column of the trial balance.
4. Double entry bookkeeping results in a system where the sum of all the debits is equal to the sum of all the credits.
5. The ledger is numbered like a textbook.

6. Withdrawals are always increased by credits.

7. An expense could create a liability.

8. A shift in assets means the total of assets must change.

9. The rules of debit and credit are constantly changing.

10. The transaction analysis chart is a teaching device.

11. The chart of accounts makes locating and identifying accounts easier.

12. The left side of any account is a credit.

13. A debit means all accounts are decreasing.

14. Financial statements are prepared from a trial balance.

15. The statement of owner's equity is prepared before the income statement.

16. Liabilities increase by credits.

17. Footings aid in balancing accounts.

18. Withdrawals are listed on the income statement.

19. The balance sheet contains the old figure for capital.

20. Think of a credit as always meaning something good.

CHAPTER 2
SOLUTIONS TO SUMMARY PRACTICE TEST

Part I

1.	debits/credits	6.	chart of accounts	11.	assets
2.	credit side	7.	ledger (general)	12.	decrease
3.	debits	8.	trial balance	13.	debit
4.	footings	9.	debits	14.	shift
5.	business transactions	10.	trial balance	15.	asset

Part II

	Debit	Credit			Debit	Credit			Debit	Credit
1.	10	60	6.		10	70	11.		100	10
2.	40	50	7.		20	70	12.		20	70
3.	30	50	8.		10	20	13.		10	70
4.	80	50	9.		110	10	14.		10	20
5.	62	10	10.		30	10	15.		30	50

Part III

1.	true	6.	false	11.	true	16.	true
2.	true	7.	true	12.	false	17.	true
3.	false	8.	false	13.	false	18.	false
4.	true	9.	false	14.	true	19.	false
5.	false	10.	true	15.	false	20.	false

CONTINUING PROBLEM—ON THE JOB FOR CHAPTER 2

Cash   1000

Bal. 3,850

Accounts Receivable   1020

Supplies   1030

Bal. 250

Computer Shop Equipment   1080

Bal. 1,200

Freedman, Withdrawals   3010

Bal. 100

Office Equipment   1090

Bal. 600

Accounts Payable   2000

335   Bal.

Freedman, Capital   3000

4,500   Bal.

Utilities Expense   5030

Bal. 85

Service Revenue   4000

1,650   Bal.

Advertising Expense   5010

Rent Expense   5020

Bal. 400

Postage Expense   5070

Phone Expense   5040

Supplies Expense   5050

Insurance Expense   5060

SANCHEZ COMPUTER CENTER
TRIAL BALANCE
AUGUST 31, 201X

	Dr.	Cr.

SANCHEZ COMPUTER CENTER
INCOME STATEMENT
FOR THE TWO MONTHS ENDED AUGUST 31, 201X

SANCHEZ COMPUTER CENTER
STATEMENT OF OWNER'S EQUITY
FOR THE TWO MONTHS ENDED AUGUST 31, 201X

SANCHEZ COMPUTER CENTER
BALANCE SHEET
AUGUST 31, 201X

ASSETS   **LIABILITIES AND OWNER'S EQUITY**

Beginning the Accounting Cycle: Journalizing, Posting, and the Trial Balance

INSTANT REPLAY: SELF-REVIEW QUIZ 3-1

LOWE'S REPAIR SERVICE
GENERAL JOURNAL

PAGE 1

Date	Account Titles and Description	PR	Dr.	Cr.

LOWE'S REPAIR SERVICE
GENERAL JOURNAL

PAGE 1 (Cont.)

Date	Account Titles and Description	PR	Dr.	Cr.

INSTANT REPLAY: SELF-REVIEW QUIZ 3-2

CLARK'S WORD PROCESSING SERVICES
GENERAL JOURNAL

PAGE 1

Date 201X		Account Titles and Description	PR		Dr.					Cr.			
May	1	Cash		10	0	0	0	00					
		Brenda Clark, Capital							10	0	0	0	00
		Initial investment of cash by owner											
	1	Word Processing Equipment		6	0	0	0	00					
		Cash							1	0	0	0	00
		Accounts Payable							5	0	0	0	00
		Purchase of equip. from Ben Co.											
	1	Prepaid Rent		1	2	0	0	00					
		Cash							1	2	0	0	00
		Rent paid in advance (3 months)											
	3	Office Supplies			6	0	0	00					
		Accounts Payable								6	0	0	00
		Purchase of supplies on acct. from Norris											
	7	Cash		3	0	0	0	00					
		Word Processing Fees							3	0	0	0	00
		Cash received for services rendered											
	13	Office Salaries Expense			6	5	0	00					
		Cash								6	5	0	00
		Payment of office salaries											
	18	Advertising Expense			2	5	0	00					
		Accounts Payable								2	5	0	00
		Bill received but not paid from Al's News											
	20	Brenda Clark, Withdrawals			6	2	5	00					
		Cash								6	2	5	00
		Personal withdrawal of cash											
	22	Accounts Receivable		5	0	0	0	00					
		Word Processing Fees							5	0	0	0	00
		Billed Morris Co. for fees earned											

CLARK'S WORD PROCESSING SERVICES
GENERAL JOURNAL

PAGE 2

Date 201X		Account Titles and Description	PR			Dr.					Cr.		
May	27	Office Salaries Expense			6	5	0	00					
		Cash								6	5	0	00
		Payment of office salaries											
	28	Accounts Payable	2		5	0	0	00					
		Cash							2	5	0	0	00
		Paid half the amount owed Ben Co.											
	29	Telephone Expense			2	2	0	00					
		Cash								2	2	0	00
		Paid telephone bill											

PARTIAL LEDGER OF CLARK'S WORD PROCESSING SERVICE

CASH   ACCOUNT NO. 111

Date	Explanation	Post Ref.	Debit	Credit	Balance Debit	Balance Credit

ACCOUNTS RECEIVABLE   ACCOUNT NO. 112

Date	Explanation	Post Ref.	Debit	Credit	Balance Debit	Balance Credit

OFFICE SUPPLIES   ACCOUNT NO. 114

Date		Explanation	Post Ref.	Debit	Credit	Balance	
						Debit	Credit

PREPAID RENT   ACCOUNT NO. 115

Date		Explanation	Post Ref.	Debit	Credit	Balance	
						Debit	Credit

WORD PROCESSING EQUIPMENT   ACCOUNT NO. 121

Date		Explanation	Post Ref.	Debit	Credit	Balance	
						Debit	Credit

ACCOUNTS PAYABLE   ACCOUNT NO. 211

Date		Explanation	Post Ref.	Debit	Credit	Balance	
						Debit	Credit

BRENDA CLARK, CAPITAL   ACCOUNT NO. 311

Date		Explanation	Post Ref.	Debit	Credit	Balance	
						Debit	Credit

BRENDA CLARK, WITHDRAWALS   ACCOUNT NO. 312

Date		Explanation	Post Ref.	Debit	Credit	Balance	
						Debit	Credit

WORD PROCESSING FEES   ACCOUNT NO. 411

Date		Explanation	Post Ref.	Debit	Credit	Balance	
						Debit	Credit

OFFICE SALARIES EXPENSE   ACCOUNT NO. 511

Date		Explanation	Post Ref.	Debit	Credit	Balance	
						Debit	Credit

ADVERTISING EXPENSE   **ACCOUNT NO. 512**

Date		Explanation	Post Ref.	Debit	Credit	Balance	
						Debit	Credit

TELEPHONE EXPENSE   **ACCOUNT NO. 513**

Date		Explanation	Post Ref.	Debit	Credit	Balance	
						Debit	Credit

INSTANT REPLAY: SELF-REVIEW QUIZ 3-3

1. _____

_____

_____

GENERAL JOURNAL

2.   PAGE 4

Date	Account Titles and Description	PR	Dr.			Cr.		

FORMS FOR DEMONSTRATION PROBLEM
(A, B)

ABBY'S EMPLOYMENT AGENCY
GENERAL JOURNAL

PAGE 1

Date	Account Titles and Description	PR	Dr.	Cr.

FORMS FOR DEMONSTRATION PROBLEM

FORMS FOR DEMONSTRATION PROBLEM (CONTINUED)

GENERAL LEDGER OF ABBY'S EMPLOYMENT AGENCY

CASH   ACCOUNT NO. 111

Date	Explanation	Post Ref.	Debit	Credit	Balance Debit	Balance Credit

ACCOUNTS RECEIVABLE   ACCOUNT NO. 112

Date	Explanation	Post Ref.	Debit	Credit	Balance Debit	Balance Credit

SUPPLIES   ACCOUNT NO. 131

Date	Explanation	Post Ref.	Debit	Credit	Balance Debit	Balance Credit

EQUIPMENT   ACCOUNT NO. 141

Date	Explanation	Post Ref.	Debit	Credit	Balance Debit	Balance Credit

FORMS FOR DEMONSTRATION PROBLEM (CONTINUED)

ACCOUNTS PAYABLE　　　　　　　　　　**ACCOUNT NO. 211**

Date	Explanation	Post Ref.	Debit	Credit	Balance Debit	Credit

A. TODD, CAPITAL　　　　　　　　　　**ACCOUNT NO. 311**

Date	Explanation	Post Ref.	Debit	Credit	Balance Debit	Credit

A. TODD, WITHDRAWALS　　　　　　　　　　**ACCOUNT NO. 321**

Date	Explanation	Post Ref.	Debit	Credit	Balance Debit	Credit

EMPLOYMENT FEES EARNED　　　　　　　　　　**ACCOUNT NO. 411**

Date	Explanation	Post Ref.	Debit	Credit	Balance Debit	Credit

FORMS FOR DEMONSTRATION PROBLEM (CONTINUED)

WAGE EXPENSE   ACCOUNT NO. 511

Date		Explanation	Post Ref.	Debit	Credit	Balance	
						Debit	Credit

TELEPHONE EXPENSE   ACCOUNT NO. 521

Date		Explanation	Post Ref.	Debit	Credit	Balance	
						Debit	Credit

ADVERTISING EXPENSE   ACCOUNT NO. 531

Date		Explanation	Post Ref.	Debit	Credit	Balance	
						Debit	Credit

END OF CHAPTER PROBLEMS

PROBLEM 3A-1 OR PROBLEM 3B-1

JAROME'S CLEANING SERVICE
GENERAL JOURNAL

PAGE 1

Date	Account Titles and Description	PR	Dr.	Cr.

PROBLEM 3A-1 OR PROBLEM 3B-1 (CONCLUDED)

JAROME'S CLEANING SERVICE
GENERAL JOURNAL

PAGE 2

Date	Account Titles and Description	PR	Dr.	Cr.

PROBLEM 3A-2 OR PROBLEM 3B-2
(A, B)

BARBIE'S ART STUDIO
GENERAL JOURNAL

PAGE 1

Date		Account Titles and Description	PR	Dr.		Cr.	

PROBLEM 3A-2 OR PROBLEM 3B-2 (CONTINUED)

GENERAL LEDGER OF BARBIE'S ART STUDIO

CASH   ACCOUNT NO. 111

Date	Explanation	Post Ref.	Debit	Credit	Balance Debit	Balance Credit

ACCOUNTS RECEIVABLE   ACCOUNT NO. 112

Date	Explanation	Post Ref.	Debit	Credit	Balance Debit	Balance Credit

PREPAID RENT   ACCOUNT NO. 114

Date	Explanation	Post Ref.	Debit	Credit	Balance Debit	Balance Credit

ART SUPPLIES   ACCOUNT NO. 121

Date	Explanation	Post Ref.	Debit	Credit	Balance Debit	Balance Credit

PROBLEM 3A-2 OR PROBLEM 3B-2 (CONTINUED)

EQUIPMENT   ACCOUNT NO. 131

Date		Explanation	Post Ref.	Debit	Credit	Balance	
						Debit	Credit

ACCOUNTS PAYABLE   ACCOUNT NO. 211

Date		Explanation	Post Ref.	Debit	Credit	Balance	
						Debit	Credit

BARBIE RILEY, CAPITAL   ACCOUNT NO. 311

Date		Explanation	Post Ref.	Debit	Credit	Balance	
						Debit	Credit

BARBIE RILEY, WITHDRAWALS   ACCOUNT NO. 312

Date		Explanation	Post Ref.	Debit	Credit	Balance	
						Debit	Credit

PROBLEM 3A-2 OR PROBLEM 3B-2 (CONTINUED)

ART FEES EARNED   ACCOUNT NO. 411

Date	Explanation	Post Ref.	Debit	Credit	Balance Debit	Balance Credit

ELECTRICAL EXPENSE   ACCOUNT NO. 511

Date	Explanation	Post Ref.	Debit	Credit	Balance Debit	Balance Credit

SALARIES EXPENSE   ACCOUNT NO. 521

Date	Explanation	Post Ref.	Debit	Credit	Balance Debit	Balance Credit

TELEPHONE EXPENSE   ACCOUNT NO. 531

Date	Explanation	Post Ref.	Debit	Credit	Balance Debit	Balance Credit

PROBLEM 3A-2 OR PROBLEM 3B-2 (CONCLUDED)

(C)

BARBIE'S ART STUDIO
TRIAL BALANCE
NOVEMBER 30, 201X

		Dr.	Cr.

PROBLEM 3A-3 OR PROBLEM 3B-3
(A, B)

A. GLOVER'S PLACEMENT AGENCY
GENERAL JOURNAL

PAGE 1

Date		Account Titles and Description	PR	Dr.		Cr.	

PROBLEM 3A-3 OR PROBLEM 3B-3 (CONTINUED)

GENERAL LEDGER OF A. GLOVER'S PLACEMENT AGENCY

CASH   **ACCOUNT NO. 111**

Date	Explanation	Post Ref.	Debit	Credit	Balance Debit	Balance Credit

ACCOUNTS RECEIVABLE   **ACCOUNT NO. 112**

Date	Explanation	Post Ref.	Debit	Credit	Balance Debit	Balance Credit

SUPPLIES   **ACCOUNT NO. 131**

Date	Explanation	Post Ref.	Debit	Credit	Balance Debit	Balance Credit

EQUIPMENT   **ACCOUNT NO. 141**

Date	Explanation	Post Ref.	Debit	Credit	Balance Debit	Balance Credit

PROBLEM 3A-3 OR PROBLEM 3B-3 (CONTINUED)

ACCOUNTS PAYABLE   ACCOUNT NO. 211

Date	Explanation	Post Ref.	Debit	Credit	Balance Debit	Balance Credit

A. GLOVER, CAPITAL   ACCOUNT NO. 311

Date	Explanation	Post Ref.	Debit	Credit	Balance Debit	Balance Credit

A. GLOVER, WITHDRAWALS   ACCOUNT NO. 312

Date	Explanation	Post Ref.	Debit	Credit	Balance Debit	Balance Credit

PLACEMENT FEES EARNED   ACCOUNT NO. 411

Date	Explanation	Post Ref.	Debit	Credit	Balance Debit	Balance Credit

PROBLEM 3A-3 OR PROBLEM 3B-3 (CONTINUED)

WAGE EXPENSE   ACCOUNT NO. 511

Date	Explanation	Post Ref.	Debit	Credit	Balance Debit	Credit

TELEPHONE EXPENSE   ACCOUNT NO. 521

Date	Explanation	Post Ref.	Debit	Credit	Balance Debit	Credit

ADVERTISING EXPENSE   ACCOUNT NO. 531

Date	Explanation	Post Ref.	Debit	Credit	Balance Debit	Credit

PROBLEM 3A-3 OR PROBLEM 3B-3 (CONCLUDED)

(C)

A. GLOVER'S PLACEMENT AGENCY
TRIAL BALANCE
NOVEMBER 30, 201X

		Dr.	Cr.

CHAPTER 3
SUMMARY PRACTICE TEST:
BEGINNING THE ACCOUNTING CYCLE: JOURNALIZING, POSTING, AND THE TRIAL BALANCE

Part I Instructions

Fill in the blank(s) to complete the statement.

1. A fiscal year runs for _____ months.
2. _____ _____ are prepared for parts of a fiscal year (monthly, quarterly, etc.).
3. The _____ _____ _____ eliminates the need for footings.
4. The positive balance of each account is referred to as its _____ _____.
5. The process of recording transactions in a journal is called _____.
6. Entries are journalized in _____ _____.
7. A ledger is often called a(n) _____ _____ _____ _____ .
8. The _____ portion of a journal entry is indented and placed below the _____ portion.
9. A journal entry requiring three or more accounts is called a(n) _____ _____ _____ .
10. Accounts receivable is a(n) _____ on the balance sheet.
11. When supplies are used up or consumed they become a(n) _____.
12. The book of original entry usually refers to a(n) _____.
13. The process of transferring information from a journal to a ledger is called _____.
14. _____ _____ deals with the process of updating the PR of the journal from the account number of the ledger to indicate to which account in the ledger information has been posted.
15. Recording $995.00 as $99.50 is an example of a(n) _____.

Part II Instructions

Match the term in column A to the definition, example, or phrase in column B. Be sure to use a letter only once.

COLUMN A	COLUMN B
__g__ 1. EXAMPLE: Book of original entry	a. 243 — 2430
_____ 2. Non-Business Expense	b. Transferring information from a general journal to a ledger
_____ 3. Slide	c. Chronological order
_____ 4. Transposition	d. Increased by a credit
_____ 5. Posting	e. Withdrawal
_____ 6. General Journal	f. Compound journal entry
_____ 7. Cross-reference	g. General journal
_____ 8. Journalizing	h. Rearrangement of digits of a number by accident
_____ 9. Balance Sheet prepared monthly	i. Updating PR column of journal from ledger account
_____ 10. A fiscal year	j. Trial balance
	k. Place to record transactions
	l. Accounting cycle
	m. Accounting period
	n. Interim statements

Part III Instructions

Answer true or false to the following statements.

1. A slide cannot affect position of numbers.
2. The totals of a trial balance may possibly not balance due to transpositions.
3. Withdrawals has a normal balance of a credit.
4. The running balance of an account can be kept in a four-column account.
5. The journal links debits and credits in alphabetical order.
6. The ledger accumulates information from the journal.
7. The post reference column of a ledger records the account number of that account.
8. An accounting cycle must be from January 1 to December 31.
9. The ledger is the book of original entry.
10. The income statement is prepared for a specific accounting period.
11. Interim statements are prepared for an entire fiscal year.
12. A calendar year could be a fiscal year.
13. 390 written by mistake as 3,900 is an example of a slide.

14. If the totals of a trial balance balance, the individual balance of items must be correct.

15. The equality of debits and credits on a trial balance does not guarantee that transactions have been properly recorded.

16. The trial balance is prepared from the journal.

17. Cross-referencing means never updating the post reference column of the journal.

18. Journals and ledgers are always in the same book.

19. The normal balance of each account is located on the same side that increases the acccount.

20. Ruling of four-column accounts is eliminated.

CHAPTER 3
SOLUTIONS TO SUMMARY PRACTICE TEST

Part I

1. 12
2. Interim statements
3. four-column ledger
4. normal balance
5. journalizing
6. chronological order
7. book of final entry
8. credit, debit
9. compound journal entry
10. asset
11. expense
12. journal
13. posting
14. Cross-reference
15. slide

Part II

1. g
2. e
3. a
4. h
5. b
6. k
7. i
8. c
9. n
10. m

Part III

1. false
2. true
3. false
4. true
5. false
6. true
7. false
8. false
9. false
10. true
11. false
12. true
13. true
14. false
15. true
16. false
17. false
18. false
19. true
20. true

CONTINUING PROBLEM—ON THE JOB FOR CHAPTER 3

SANCHEZ COMPUTER CENTER
GENERAL JOURNAL

PAGE 1

Date	Account Titles and Description	PR	Dr.	Cr.

SANCHEZ COMPUTER CENTER
GENERAL JOURNAL

PAGE 1 (Cont.)

Date	Account Titles and Description	PR	Dr.	Cr.

CASH   **ACCOUNT NO. 1000**

Date		Explanation	Post Ref.	Debit					Credit					Balance									
														Debit						Credit				
9/1	1X	Balance forward	✔											2	8	6	5	00						

ACCOUNTS RECEIVABLE ACCOUNT NO. 1020

Date		Explanation	Post Ref.	Debit	Credit	Balance	
						Debit	Credit
9/1	1X	Balance forward	✔			8 5 0 00	

PREPAID RENT ACCOUNT NO. 1025

Date	Explanation	Post Ref.	Debit	Credit	Balance	
					Debit	Credit

SUPPLIES ACCOUNT NO. 1030

Date	Explanation	Post Ref.	Debit	Credit	Balance	
					Debit	Credit
9/1	Balance forward	✔			4 5 0 00	

COMPUTER SHOP EQUIPMENT ACCOUNT NO. 1080

Date		Explanation	Post Ref.	Debit	Credit	Balance	
						Debit	Credit
9/1	1X		✔			1 2 0 0 00	

OFFICE EQUIPMENT   ACCOUNT NO. 1090

Date		Explanation	Post Ref.	Debit	Credit	Balance	
						Debit	Credit
9/1	1X	Balance forward	✔			6 0 0 00	

ACCOUNTS PAYABLE   ACCOUNT NO. 2000

Date		Explanation	Post Ref.	Debit	Credit	Balance	
						Debit	Credit
9/1	1X	Balance forward	✔				4 0 5 00

FREEDMAN, CAPITAL   ACCOUNT NO. 3000

Date		Explanation	Post Ref.	Debit	Credit	Balance	
						Debit	Credit
9/1	1X	Balance forward	✔				4 5 0 0 00

FREEDMAN, WITHDRAWALS   ACCOUNT NO. 3010

Date		Explanation	Post Ref.	Debit	Credit	Balance	
						Debit	Credit
9/1	1X	Balance forward	✔			1 0 0 00	

SERVICE REVENUE   ACCOUNT NO. **4000**

Date		Explanation	Post Ref.	Debit	Credit	Balance	
						Debit	Credit
9/1	1X	Balance forward	✔				3 4 0 0 00

ADVERTISING EXPENSE   ACCOUNT NO. **5010**

Date		Explanation	Post Ref.	Debit	Credit	Balance	
						Debit	Credit
9/1	1X	Balance forward	✔			1 4 0 0 00	

RENT EXPENSE   ACCOUNT NO. **5020**

Date		Explanation	Post Ref.	Debit	Credit	Balance	
						Debit	Credit
9/1	1X	Balance forward	✔			4 0 0 00	

UTILITIES EXPENSE   ACCOUNT NO. 5030

Date		Explanation	Post Ref.	Debit	Credit	Balance	
						Debit	Credit
9/1	1X	Balance forward	✔			8 5 00	

PHONE EXPENSE   ACCOUNT NO. 5040

Date		Explanation	Post Ref.	Debit	Credit	Balance	
						Debit	Credit
9/1	1X	Balance forward	✔			1 5 5 00	

SUPPLIES EXPENSE   ACCOUNT NO. 5050

Date		Explanation	Post Ref.	Debit	Credit	Balance	
						Debit	Credit

The Accounting Cycle Continued: Preparing Worksheets and Financial Statements

INSTANT REPLAY: SELF-REVIEW QUIZ 4-1

Use one of the blank fold-out worksheets that accompanied your textbook.

INSTANT REPLAY: SELF-REVIEW QUIZ 4-2

(1) _____

(2) _____

(3)

LIABILITIES AND OWNER'S EQUITY

ASSETS

FORMS FOR DEMONSTRATION PROBLEM

(1)

Use one of the blank fold-out worksheets that accompanied your textbook.

(2)

FROST COMPANY
INCOME STATEMENT
FOR MONTH ENDED DECEMBER 31, 201X

(2)

FROST COMPANY
STATEMENT OF OWNER'S EQUITY
FOR MONTH ENDED DECEMBER 31, 201X

DEMONSTRATION PROBLEM (CONCLUDED)

(2)

FROST COMPANY
BALANCE SHEET
DECEMBER 31, 201X

ASSETS

LIABILITIES AND OWNER'S EQUITY

CHAPTER 4
CONCEPT CHECK

1. A. _____
_____
_____

B.

1. Accounts Affected	2. Category	3. ↑ ↓	4. Rules	5. T Account

C. _____
_____
_____
_____
_____

2. A. _____
_____
_____
_____

B.

1. Accounts Affected	2. Category	3. ↑ ↓	4. Rules	5. T Account

C. _____
_____

3. A. _____
B. _____
C.

1. Accounts Affected	2. Category	3. ↑ ↓	4. Rules	5. T Account

D. _____
_____
_____

4. A.

1. Accounts Affected	2. Category	3. ↑ ↓	4. Rules	5. T Account

B. _____
_____

5.

A. _____   H. _____
B. _____   I. _____
C. _____   J. _____
D. _____   K. _____
E. _____   L. _____
F. _____   M. _____
G. _____   N. _____

6.

A. _____
_____
_____

B. _____
_____
_____
_____
_____

FORMS FOR EXERCISES A OR B

4A-1 OR 4B-1

Account	Category	Normal Balance	Financial Statement(s) Found on

4A-2 OR 4B-2

Accounts Affected	Category	↑ ↓	Rules	Amount
A.				
B.				

4A-3 OR 4B-3

A. _____

B. _____

_____

_____

4A-4 OR 4B-4

Use one of the blank fold-out worksheets that accompanied your textbook.

EXERCISES (CONTINUED)

4A-5 OR 4B-5

(A)

J. TRIPP
INCOME STATEMENT
FOR MONTH ENDED OCTOBER 31, 201X

(B)

J. TRIPP
STATEMENT OF OWNER'S EQUITY
FOR MONTH ENDED OCTOBER 31, 201X

EXERCISES (CONCLUDED)
(C)

J. TRIPP
BALANCE SHEET
OCTOBER 31, 201X

LIABILITIES AND OWNER'S EQUITY

ASSETS

CHAPTER 4
SUMMARY PRACTICE TEST:
THE ACCOUNTING CYCLE CONTINUED:
PREPARING WORKSHEETS AND FINANCIAL STATEMENTS

Part I Instructions

Fill in the blank(s) to complete the statement.

1. _____ is an estimate.
2. A(n) _____ will decrease accumulated depreciation.
3. _____ affect both the income statement and balance sheet.
4. The adjustment for supplies reflects the amount of supplies _____ _____.
5. Supplies Expense is found on the income statement. Supplies are found on the _____ _____.
6. _____ _____ reflects the cost of equipment at time of purchase.
7. Depreciation Expense is found on the _____ _____.
8. _____ _____ is a contra asset that has a credit balance.
9. Accumulated Depreciation, a contra asset, is found on the _____ _____.
10. Historical or original cost of an auto less _____ _____ reflects the unused amount of the auto on the accounting books.
11. Withdrawals are found in the _____ column of the balance sheet section of the worksheet.
12. Salaries Payable is a liability that will appear in the _____ _____ _____ _____ of the worksheet.
13. The figure for net income on the worksheet is carried over to the _____ column of the balance sheet.
14. A worksheet is a(n) _____ report.
15. _____ _____ are prepared after the completion of the worksheet.

Part II Instructions

Complete the following statements by circling the letter of the appropriate answer.

1.   The adjustment for depreciation results in Accumulated Depreciation

    a. decreasing.

    b. staying the same.

    c. increasing.

2.   The historical or original cost of an asset on the worksheet

    a. never changes.

    b. sometimes changes.

    c. continually changes.

3.   Net income on the worksheet is carried over to the

    a. trial balance.

    b. adjusted trial balance.

    c. balance sheet column.

4.   Accumulated Depreciation is found on

    a. a worksheet.

    b. an income statement.

    c. both a worksheet and an income statement.

5.   Accumulated Depreciation, a contra asset, is increased by a

    a. debit.

    b. credit.

    c. both a and b.

6.   A worksheet is usually completed

    a. one column at a time.

    b. two columns at a time.

    c. three columns at a time.

7.   Withdrawals on the worksheet are found in the

    a. debit column of the income statement.

    b. debit column of the balance sheet.

    c. both a and b.

8.   The worksheet specifically shows the

    a. beginning figure for owner capital.

    b. ending figure for owner capital.

    c. average figure for owner capital.

9.   The total of the assets on a formal balance sheet will _____ equal the total of the debit column of the balance sheet on the worksheet.

    a. always

    b. sometimes

    c. never

10. The adjustment for depreciation affects

    a. the income statement.

    b. the balance sheet.

    c. both a and b.

11. The adjustment for supplies requires one to know

    a. beginning supplies plus supplies purchased.

    b. supplies on hand.

    c. both a and b.

12. The purpose of adjustments is to
- a. bring general journals up to date.
- b. bring ledger accounts up to proper balances in the journal.
- c. bring ledger accounts to proper balance.

13. Book values equals cost less
- a. expenses.
- b. accumulated depreciation.
- c. neither a nor b.

14. The _____ is an informal report.
- a. income statement
- b. balance sheet
- c. worksheet

Part III Instructions

Answer true or false to the following statements.

1. The normal balance of accumulated depreciation is a credit.
2. Liabilities are only income statement accounts.
3. The total of the adjustments column may balance but be incorrect.
4. Prepaid rent is found on the income statement.
5. Rent expense is found on the income statement.
6. Debits and credits are found on financial statements.
7. Historical cost relates only to automobiles.
8. Accumulated Depreciation is found on the income statement.
9. As Accumulated Depreciation increases, the historical cost changes.
10. The adjustment for depreciation directly affects cash.
11. An expense is only recorded when it is paid.
12. The ending figure for owner capital does not have to be calculated from the worksheet.
13. Withdrawals have the same balance as Accumulated Depreciation.
14. Salaries Payable is an asset on the income statement.
15. Net loss would never be shown on a worksheet.
16. The net income on the worksheet is the same amount on the income statement.
17. Worksheets must use dollar signs.
18. The worksheet eliminates the need to prepare financial statements.
19. Cost less accumulated depreciation equals book value.
20. Accrued Salaries are expenses that have already been paid for.

CHAPTER 4
SOLUTIONS TO SUMMARY PRACTICE TEST

Part I

1. Depreciation
2. debit
3. Adjustments
4. used up
5. balance sheet
6. Historical (original) cost
7. income statement
8. Accumulated Depreciation
9. balance sheet
10. accumulated depreciation
11. debit
12. balance sheet credit column
13. credit
14. informal
15. Financial statements

Part II

1. c
2. a
3. c
4. a
5. b
6. b
7. b
8. a
9. c
10. c
11. c
12. c
13. b
14. c

Part III

1. true
2. false
3. true
4. false
5. true
6. false
7. false
8. false
9. false
10. false
11. false
12. true
13. false
14. false
15. false
16. true
17. false
18. false
19. true
20. false

CONTINUING PROBLEM—ON THE JOB FOR CHAPTER 4*

SANCHEZ COMPUTER CENTER
INCOME STATEMENT
FOR THE THREE MONTHS ENDED SEPTEMBER 30, 201X

SANCHEZ COMPUTER CENTER
STATEMENT OF OWNER'S EQUITY
FOR THE THREE MONTHS ENDED SEPTEMBER 30, 201X

*Use one of the blank fold-out worksheets that accompanied your textbook.

Name _____ Class _____ Date _____

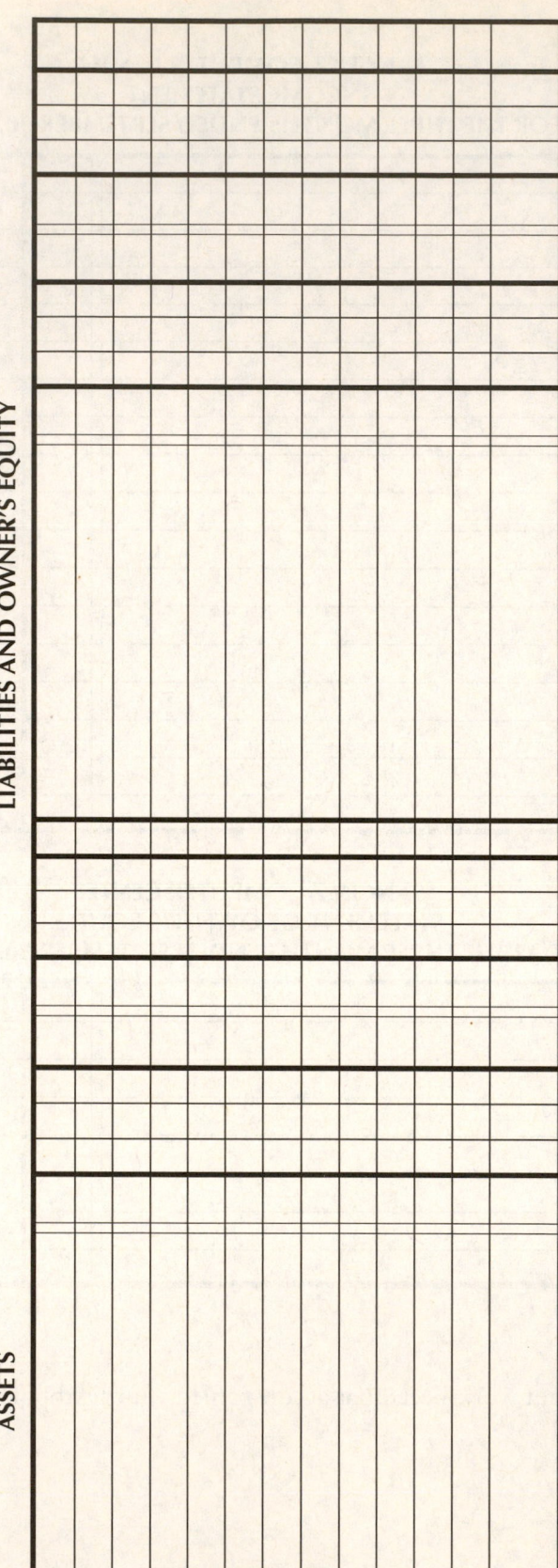

SANCHEZ COMPUTER CENTER
BALANCE SHEET
SEPTEMBER 30, 201X

ASSETS

LIABILITIES AND OWNER'S EQUITY

THE ACCOUNTING CYCLE COMPLETED: ADJUSTING, CLOSING, AND THE POST-CLOSING TRIAL BALANCE

INSTANT REPLAY: SELF-REVIEW QUIZ 5-1

(1)

Date	Account Titles and Description	PR	Dr.	Cr.

(2) Partial Ledger

Depreciation Expense,
Store Equipment   511

Accumulated Depreciation,
Store Equipment   122

4

Prepaid Insurance   116

3

Insurance Expense   516

Store Supplies   114

5

Supplies Expense   514

Salaries Expense   512

8

Salaries Payable   212

INSTANT REPLAY: SELF-REVIEW QUIZ 5-2
(1) _____

_____
_____

P. Logan, Capital 310	Revenue from Clients 410	Supplies Expense 514
14	25	4

P. Logan, Withdrawals 311	Depreciation Expense, Store Equipment 510	Insurance Expense 516
3	1	2

Income Summary 312	Salaries Expense 512	Rent Expense 518
	11	2

_____
_____
_____

INSTANT REPLAY: SELF-REVIEW QUIZ 5-3

_____
_____

FORMS FOR DEMONSTRATION PROBLEM

Use one of the blank fold-out worksheets that accompanied your textbook.

ROLO COMPANY
GENERAL JOURNAL

PAGE 1

Date	Account Titles and Description	PR	Dr.	Cr.

Name _____ Class _____ Date _____

FORMS FOR DEMONSTRATION PROBLEM (CONTINUED)

ROLO COMPANY
GENERAL JOURNAL

PAGE 2

Date	Account Titles and Description	PR	Dr.	Cr.

FORMS FOR DEMONSTRATION PROBLEM (CONTINUED)

CASH   ACCOUNT NO. 111

Date	Explanation	Post Ref.	Debit	Credit	Balance	
					Debit	Credit

ACCOUNTS RECEIVABLE   ACCOUNT NO. 112

Date	Explanation	Post Ref.	Debit	Credit	Balance	
					Debit	Credit

PREPAID RENT   ACCOUNT NO. 114

Date	Explanation	Post Ref.	Debit	Credit	Balance	
					Debit	Credit

OFFICE SUPPLIES   ACCOUNT NO. 115

Date	Explanation	Post Ref.	Debit	Credit	Balance	
					Debit	Credit

FORMS FOR DEMONSTRATION PROBLEM (CONTINUED)

OFFICE EQUIPMENT   ACCOUNT NO. 121

Date		Explanation	Post Ref.	Debit	Credit	Balance	
						Debit	Credit

ACCUMULATED DEPRECIATION, OFFICE EQUIPMENT   ACCOUNT NO. 122

Date		Explanation	Post Ref.	Debit	Credit	Balance	
						Debit	Credit

ACCOUNTS PAYABLE   ACCOUNT NO. 211

Date		Explanation	Post Ref.	Debit	Credit	Balance	
						Debit	Credit

FORMS FOR DEMONSTRATION PROBLEM (CONTINUED)

SALARIES PAYABLE   **ACCOUNT NO. 212**

Date	Explanation	Post Ref.	Debit	Credit	Balance	
					Debit	Credit

ROLO KERN, CAPITAL   **ACCOUNT NO. 311**

Date	Explanation	Post Ref.	Debit	Credit	Balance	
					Debit	Credit

ROLO KERN, WITHDRAWALS   **ACCOUNT NO. 312**

Date	Explanation	Post Ref.	Debit	Credit	Balance	
					Debit	Credit

INCOME SUMMARY   **ACCOUNT NO. 313**

Date	Explanation	Post Ref.	Debit	Credit	Balance	
					Debit	Credit

FEES EARNED   **ACCOUNT NO. 411**

Date	Explanation	Post Ref.	Debit	Credit	Balance	
					Debit	Credit

FORMS FOR DEMONSTRATION PROBLEM (CONTINUED)

SALARIES EXPENSE   ACCOUNT NO. 511

Date		Explanation	Post Ref.	Debit	Credit	Balance	
						Debit	Credit

ADVERTISING EXPENSE   ACCOUNT NO. 512

Date		Explanation	Post Ref.	Debit	Credit	Balance	
						Debit	Credit

RENT EXPENSE   ACCOUNT NO. 513

Date		Explanation	Post Ref.	Debit	Credit	Balance	
						Debit	Credit

OFFICE SUPPLIES EXPENSE   ACCOUNT NO. 514

Date		Explanation	Post Ref.	Debit	Credit	Balance	
						Debit	Credit

DEPRECIATION EXPENSE, OFFICE EQUIPMENT   ACCOUNT NO. 515

Date		Explanation	Post Ref.	Debit	Credit	Balance	
						Debit	Credit

FORMS FOR DEMONSTRATION PROBLEM (CONTINUED)

ROLO COMPANY
INCOME STATEMENT
FOR MONTH ENDED JANUARY 31, 201X

ROLO COMPANY
STATEMENT OF OWNER'S EQUITY
FOR MONTH ENDED JANUARY 31, 201X

FORMS FOR DEMONSTRATION PROBLEM (CONTINUED)

ROLO COMPANY
BALANCE SHEET
JANUARY 31, 201X

ASSETS

LIABILITIES AND OWNER'S EQUITY

FORMS FOR DEMONSTRATION PROBLEM (CONCLUDED)

ROLO COMPANY
POST-CLOSING TRIAL BALANCE
JANUARY 31, 201X

	Dr.	Cr.

CHAPTER 5
CONCEPT CHECK

GENERAL JOURNAL

1.

PAGE 3

Date	Account Titles and Description	PR	Dr.	Cr.

Prepaid Insurance   115   Insurance Expense   510

Store Supplies   116   Depreciation Expense,
                                   Store Equipment   512

Accumulated Depreciation
Store Equipment   119   Supplies Expense   514

Salaries Payable   210   Salaries Expense   516

2. _____

_____

_____

_____

_____

_____

_____

_____

GENERAL JOURNAL

3.

PAGE 4

Date		Account Titles and Description	PR		Dr.		Cr.	

4.

Income Summary   314

5.

Max Benson, Capital   310

FORMS FOR EXERCISES A OR B

5A-1 OR 5B-1

Date		Account Titles and Description	PR		Dr.		Cr.

5A-2 OR 5B-2

	TEMPORARY	PERMANENT	WILL BE CLOSED

1.

2.

3.

4.

5.

6.

7.

EXERCISES (CONTINUED)

5A-3 OR 5B-3

Date		Account Titles and Description	PR	Dr.	Cr.

EXERCISES (CONCLUDED)

5A-4 OR 5B-4

Date		Account Titles and Description	PR	Dr.	Cr.

5A-5 OR 5B-5

WINTER CO.
POST-CLOSING TRIAL BALANCE
OCTOBER 31, 201X

		Dr.	Cr.

END OF CHAPTER PROBLEMS

PROBLEM 5A-1 OR PROBLEM 5B-1

Use one of the blank fold-out worksheets that accompanied your textbook.

(2)

DAISY'S DANCE STUDIO
GENERAL JOURNAL

PAGE 3

Date	Account Titles and Description	PR	Dr.	Cr.

PROBLEM 5A-2 OR PROBLEM 5B-2

(1)

PALMER'S CLEANING SERVICE
GENERAL JOURNAL

PAGE 2

Date	Account Titles and Description	PR	Dr.	Cr.

PROBLEM 5A-2 OR PROBLEM 5B-2 (CONTINUED)

CASH   ACCOUNT NO. 112

Date		Explanation	Post Ref.	Debit	Credit	Balance	
						Debit	Credit

PREPAID INSURANCE   ACCOUNT NO. 114

Date		Explanation	Post Ref.	Debit	Credit	Balance	
						Debit	Credit

CLEANING SUPPLIES   ACCOUNT NO. 115

Date		Explanation	Post Ref.	Debit	Credit	Balance	
						Debit	Credit

AUTO   ACCOUNT NO. 121

Date		Explanation	Post Ref.	Debit	Credit	Balance	
						Debit	Credit

ACCUMULATED DEPRECIATION, AUTO   ACCOUNT NO. 122

Date		Explanation	Post Ref.	Debit	Credit	Balance	
						Debit	Credit

PROBLEM 5A-2 OR PROBLEM 5B-2 (CONTINUED)

ACCOUNTS PAYABLE   ACCOUNT NO. 212

Date		Explanation	Post Ref.	Debit	Credit	Balance	
						Debit	Credit

SALARIES PAYABLE   ACCOUNT NO. 213

Date		Explanation	Post Ref.	Debit	Credit	Balance	
						Debit	Credit

B. PALMER, CAPITAL   ACCOUNT NO. 312

Date		Explanation	Post Ref.	Debit	Credit	Balance	
						Debit	Credit

B. PALMER, WITHDRAWALS   ACCOUNT NO. 313

Date		Explanation	Post Ref.	Debit	Credit	Balance	
						Debit	Credit

INCOME SUMMARY   ACCOUNT NO. 314

Date		Explanation	Post Ref.	Debit	Credit	Balance	
						Debit	Credit

PROBLEM 5A-2 OR PROBLEM 5B-2 (CONTINUED)

CLEANING FEES   ACCOUNT NO. <u>412</u>

Date	Explanation	Post Ref.	Debit	Credit	Balance	
					Debit	Credit

SALARIES EXPENSE   ACCOUNT NO. <u>513</u>

Date	Explanation	Post Ref.	Debit	Credit	Balance	
					Debit	Credit

TELEPHONE EXPENSE   ACCOUNT NO. <u>514</u>

Date	Explanation	Post Ref.	Debit	Credit	Balance	
					Debit	Credit

ADVERTISING EXPENSE   ACCOUNT NO. <u>515</u>

Date	Explanation	Post Ref.	Debit	Credit	Balance	
					Debit	Credit

GAS EXPENSE   ACCOUNT NO. <u>516</u>

Date	Explanation	Post Ref.	Debit	Credit	Balance	
					Debit	Credit

PROBLEM 5A-2 OR PROBLEM 5B-2 (CONTINUED)

INSURANCE EXPENSE   ACCOUNT NO. 517

Date	Explanation	Post Ref.	Debit	Credit	Balance Debit	Balance Credit

CLEANING SUPPLIES EXPENSE   ACCOUNT NO. 518

Date	Explanation	Post Ref.	Debit	Credit	Balance Debit	Balance Credit

DEPRECIATION EXPENSE, AUTO   ACCOUNT NO. 519

Date	Explanation	Post Ref.	Debit	Credit	Balance Debit	Balance Credit

PROBLEM 5A-2 OR PROBLEM 5B-2 (CONCLUDED)

(2)

PALMER'S CLEANING SERVICE
POST-CLOSING TRIAL BALANCE
JANUARY 31, 201X

	Dr.	Cr.

PROBLEM 5A-3 OR PROBLEM 5B-3

Use one of the blank fold-out worksheets that accompanied your textbook.

PROBLEM 5A-3 OR PROBLEM 5B-3 (CONTINUED)

PARKER'S PLOWING
GENERAL JOURNAL

PAGE 1

Date	Account Titles and Description	PR	Dr.	Cr.

PROBLEM 5A-3 OR PROBLEM 5B-3 (CONTINUED)

**PARKER'S PLOWING
GENERAL JOURNAL**

PAGE 2

Date	Account Titles and Description	PR	Dr.	Cr.

PROBLEM 5A-3 OR PROBLEM 5B-3 (CONTINUED)

PARKER'S PLOWING
GENERAL JOURNAL

PAGE 3

Date	Account Titles and Description	PR	Dr.	Cr.

PROBLEM 5A-3 OR PROBLEM 5B-3 (CONTINUED)

CASH   ACCOUNT NO. 111

Date	Explanation	Post Ref.	Debit	Credit	Balance Debit	Balance Credit

ACCOUNTS RECEIVABLE   ACCOUNT NO. 112

Date	Explanation	Post Ref.	Debit	Credit	Balance Debit	Balance Credit

PREPAID RENT   ACCOUNT NO. 114

Date	Explanation	Post Ref.	Debit	Credit	Balance Debit	Balance Credit

SNOW SUPPLIES   ACCOUNT NO. 115

Date	Explanation	Post Ref.	Debit	Credit	Balance Debit	Balance Credit

PROBLEM 5A-3 OR PROBLEM 5B-3 (CONTINUED)

OFFICE EQUIPMENT   ACCOUNT NO. 121

Date	Explanation	Post Ref.	Debit	Credit	Balance	
					Debit	Credit

ACCUMULATED DEPRECIATION, OFFICE EQUIPMENT   ACCOUNT NO. 122

Date	Explanation	Post Ref.	Debit	Credit	Balance	
					Debit	Credit

SNOW EQUIPMENT   ACCOUNT NO. 123

Date	Explanation	Post Ref.	Debit	Credit	Balance	
					Debit	Credit

ACCUMULATED DEPRECIATION, SNOW EQUIPMENT   ACCOUNT NO. 124

Date	Explanation	Post Ref.	Debit	Credit	Balance	
					Debit	Credit

ACCOUNTS PAYABLE   ACCOUNT NO. 211

Date	Explanation	Post Ref.	Debit	Credit	Balance	
					Debit	Credit

PROBLEM 5A-3 OR PROBLEM 5B-3 (CONTINUED)

SALARIES PAYABLE   ACCOUNT NO. 212

Date		Explanation	Post Ref.	Debit	Credit	Balance	
						Debit	Credit

PARKER MURONEY, CAPITAL   ACCOUNT NO. 311

Date		Explanation	Post Ref.	Debit	Credit	Balance	
						Debit	Credit

PARKER MURONEY, WITHDRAWALS   ACCOUNT NO. 312

Date		Explanation	Post Ref.	Debit	Credit	Balance	
						Debit	Credit

INCOME SUMMARY   ACCOUNT NO. 313

Date		Explanation	Post Ref.	Debit	Credit	Balance	
						Debit	Credit

PLOWING FEES   ACCOUNT NO. 411

Date		Explanation	Post Ref.	Debit	Credit	Balance	
						Debit	Credit

PROBLEM 5A-3 OR PROBLEM 5B-3 (CONTINUED)

SALARIES EXPENSE   ACCOUNT NO. 511

Date	Explanation	Post Ref.	Debit	Credit	Balance Debit	Balance Credit

ADVERTISING EXPENSE   ACCOUNT NO. 512

Date	Explanation	Post Ref.	Debit	Credit	Balance Debit	Balance Credit

TELEPHONE EXPENSE   ACCOUNT NO. 513

Date	Explanation	Post Ref.	Debit	Credit	Balance Debit	Balance Credit

RENT EXPENSE   ACCOUNT NO. 514

Date	Explanation	Post Ref.	Debit	Credit	Balance Debit	Balance Credit

SNOW SUPPLIES EXPENSE   ACCOUNT NO. 515

Date	Explanation	Post Ref.	Debit	Credit	Balance Debit	Balance Credit

PROBLEM 5A-3 OR PROBLEM 5B-3 (CONTINUED)

DEPRECIATION EXPENSE, OFFICE EQUIPMENT   ACCOUNT NO. 516

Date	Explanation	Post Ref.	Debit	Credit	Balance Debit	Balance Credit

DEPRECIATION EXPENSE, SNOW EQUIPMENT   ACCOUNT NO. 517

Date	Explanation	Post Ref.	Debit	Credit	Balance Debit	Balance Credit

PROBLEM 5A-3 OR PROBLEM 5B-3 (CONTINUED)

PARKER'S PLOWING
INCOME STATEMENT
FOR MONTH ENDED JANUARY 31, 201X

PARKER'S PLOWING
STATEMENT OF OWNER'S EQUITY
FOR MONTH ENDED JANUARY 31, 201X

PROBLEM 5A-3 OR PROBLEM 5B-3 (CONTINUED)

PARKER'S PLOWING
BALANCE SHEET
JANUARY 31, 201X

LIABILITIES AND OWNER'S EQUITY

ASSETS

PROBLEM 5A-3 OR PROBLEM 5B-3 (CONCLUDED)

PARKER'S PLOWING
POST-CLOSING TRIAL BALANCE
JANUARY 31, 201X

		Dr.		Cr.	

CHAPTER 5
SUMMARY PRACTICE TEST:
THE ACCOUNTING CYCLE COMPLETED:
ADJUSTING, CLOSING, AND
THE POST-CLOSING TRIAL BALANCE

Part I Instructions

Fill in the blank(s) to complete the statement.

1. After the closing process only _____ accounts remain with balances.
2. Revenue, Expenses, and Withdrawals are examples of _____ _____.
3. _____ in temporary accounts will not be carried over to the next accounting period.
4. After closing entries are posted, owner's Capital in the ledger will contain the _____
   _____.
5. Revenue is closed to Income Summary by a(n) _____ to each revenue account and a(n)
   _____ to Income Summary.
6. Expenses are closed to Income Summary by _____ the individual expenses and
   _____ Income Summary.
7. If the balance of Income Summary is a credit, it will be closed by _____ Income
   Summary and _____ owner's Capital.
8. The balance of Withdrawals is closed by a(n) _____ and the amount transferred to
   owner's Capital by a(n) _____.
9. At the end of the closing process, all temporary accounts in the ledger will have a(n)
   _____ balance.
10. The _____ _____ _____ _____ contains a list
    of permanent accounts after the adjusting and closing entries have been posted to the ledger from a
    journal.
11. Closing entries can be prepared from a(n) _____.
12. After closing entries are posted, Income Summary will have a(n) _____ balance.
13. Journalizing adjustments can be done from the _____.
14. Cash, Equipment, and Supplies are not part of the _____ process.
15. Income Summary is a(n) _____ account.

Part II Instructions

The following is a chart of accounts for Al's Auto Shop. From the chart, indicate in Column B (by account number) which accounts will be debited or credited as related to the transactions in Column A.

CHART OF ACCOUNTS

ASSETS	OWNER'S EQUITY
112 Cash	340 A. Jones, Capital
114 Accounts Receivable	341 A. Jones, Withdrawals
116 Prepaid Rent	342 Income Summary
118 Auto Supplies	
120 Delivery Truck	REVENUE
121 Accumulated Depreciation, Delivery Truck	450 Fees Earned
LIABILITIES	EXPENSES
230 Accounts Payable	560 Salaries
232 Salaries Payable	562 Advertising
	564 Rent
	566 Auto Supplies
	568 Depreciation Expense, Delivery Truck

	COLUMN A	COLUMN B	
		Debit(s)	Credit(s)
1.	Closed balance in revenue account to Income Summary.	_____	_____
2.	Closed balance in individual expenses to Income Summary.	_____	_____
3.	Closed balance in Income Summary to owner's Capital. (Assume that it is a net income.)	_____	_____
4.	Closed Withdrawals to owner's Capital.	_____	_____
5.	Recorded auto supplies used up.	_____	_____
6.	Recorded depreciation on delivery truck.	_____	_____
7.	Brought Salaries Expense up to date (an adjustment).	_____	_____

Part III Instructions

Answer true or false to the following statements.

1. Closing entries are done every other month.
2. Adjustments are journalized before preparing the worksheet.
3. Closing entries can only clear permanent accounts.
4. Income summary is a temporary account.
5. Interim statements can be prepared from worksheets.
6. To clear expenses in the closing process, a compound entry is appropriate.
7. Withdrawals is a temporary account on the income statement.
8. Income Summary helps update withdrawals.

9. Accumulated Depreciation is a permanent account on the income statement.

10. Cash, Rent Expense, and Accounts Receivable need to be closed at the end of the period.

11. Closing entries do not relate to the worksheet.

12. Revenue is closed by a credit.

13. Expenses are placed on the debit side of the Income Summary account.

14. A post-closing trial balance closely resembles the ending balance sheet.

15. Accumulated Depreciation never has to be adjusted.

16. Interim statements are always prepared monthly.

17. A post-closing trial balance is prepared before adjustments are journalized.

18. Income Summary is shown on the balance sheet.

19. The process of closing entries will help update owner's Capital.

20. The normal balance of the Income Summary is a debit.

21. The normal balance of the Income Summary is a credit.

22. The income statement is listed in terms of debits and credits.

23. Closing updates only permanent accounts.

24. The completion of financial statements means that the Capital account in the ledger has been updated.

25. Withdrawals is closed to Income Summary.

SOLUTIONS TO SUMMARY PRACTICE TEST

Part I

1. permanent
2. temporary accounts
3. Balances
4. ending figure (balance)
5. debit, credit
6. crediting, debiting
7. debiting, crediting
8. credit, debit
9. zero
10. post-closing trial balance
11. worksheet
12. zero
13. worksheet
14. closing
15. temporary

Part II

	Debit	Credit
1.	450	342
2.	342	560, 562, 564, 566, 568
3.	342	340
4.	340	341
5.	566	118
6.	568	121
7.	560	232

Part III

1.	false	**7.**	false	**13.**	true	**19.**	true	**25.**	false
2.	false	**8.**	false	**14.**	true	**20.**	false		
3.	false	**9.**	false	**15.**	false	**21.**	false		
4.	true	**10.**	false	**16.**	false	**22.**	false		
5.	true	**11.**	false	**17.**	false	**23.**	false		
6.	true	**12.**	false	**18.**	false	**24.**	false		

CONTINUING PROBLEM—ON THE JOB FOR CHAPTER 5

SANCHEZ COMPUTER CENTER
GENERAL JOURNAL

PAGE 2

Date	Account Titles and Description	PR	Dr.	Cr.

CASH   ACCOUNT NO. <u>1000</u>

Date		Explanation	Post Ref.	Debit	Credit	Balance Debit	Balance Credit
9/30	1X	Balance forward	✔			1 6 4 5 00	

ACCOUNTS RECEIVABLE   ACCOUNT NO. <u>1020</u>

Date		Explanation	Post Ref.	Debit	Credit	Balance Debit	Balance Credit
9/30	1X	Balance forward	✔			2 6 0 0 00	

PREPAID RENT   ACCOUNT NO. <u>1025</u>

Date		Explanation	Post Ref.	Debit	Credit	Balance Debit	Balance Credit
9/30	1X	Balance forward	✔			1 2 0 0 00	

SUPPLIES   ACCOUNT NO. <u>1030</u>

Date		Explanation	Post Ref.	Debit	Credit	Balance Debit	Balance Credit
9/30	1X	Balance forward	✔			4 5 0 00	

COMPUTER SHOP EQUIPMENT   ACCOUNT NO. 1080

Date		Explanation	Post Ref.	Debit	Credit	Balance	
						Debit	Credit
9/30	1X	Balance forward	✔			2 4 0 0 00	

ACCUMULATED DEPRECIATION, COMPUTER SHOP EQUIPMENT   ACCOUNT NO. 1081

Date		Explanation	Post Ref.	Debit	Credit	Balance	
						Debit	Credit

OFFICE EQUIPMENT   ACCOUNT NO. 1090

Date		Explanation	Post Ref.	Debit	Credit	Balance	
						Debit	Credit
9/30	1X	Balance forward	✔			6 0 0 00	

ACCUMULATED DEPRECIATION, OFFICE EQUIPMENT   ACCOUNT NO. 1091

Date		Explanation	Post Ref.	Debit	Credit	Balance	
						Debit	Credit

ACCOUNTS PAYABLE   ACCOUNT NO. 2000

Date		Explanation	Post Ref.	Debit	Credit	Balance	
						Debit	Credit
9/30	1X	Balance forward	✔				2 1 0 00

T. FREEDMAN, CAPITAL   ACCOUNT NO. 3000

Date		Explanation	Post Ref.	Debit	Credit	Balance	
						Debit	Credit
9/30	1X	Balance forward	✔				4 5 0 0 00

T. FREEDMAN, WITHDRAWALS   ACCOUNT NO. 3010

Date		Explanation	Post Ref.	Debit	Credit	Balance	
						Debit	Credit
9/30	1X	Balance forward	✔			1 0 0 00	

INCOME SUMMARY ACCOUNT NO. 3020

Date	Explanation	Post Ref.	Debit	Credit	Balance Debit	Balance Credit

SERVICE REVENUE ACCOUNT NO. 4000

Date	Explanation	Post Ref.	Debit	Credit	Balance Debit	Balance Credit
9/30 1X	Balance forward	✔				6 6 8 5 00

ADVERTISING EXPENSE ACCOUNT NO. 5010

Date	Explanation	Post Ref.	Debit	Credit	Balance Debit	Balance Credit
9/30 1X	Balance forward	✔			1 4 0 0 00	

RENT EXPENSE ACCOUNT NO. 5020

Date	Explanation	Post Ref.	Debit	Credit	Balance Debit	Balance Credit
9/30 1X	Balance forward	✔			4 0 0 00	

UTILITIES EXPENSE   ACCOUNT NO. 5030

Date		Explanation	Post Ref.	Debit	Credit	Balance Debit	Balance Credit
9/30	1X	Balance forward	✔			1 8 0 00	

PHONE EXPENSE   ACCOUNT NO. 5040

Date		Explanation	Post Ref.	Debit	Credit	Balance Debit	Balance Credit
9/30	1X	Balance forward	✔			2 2 0 00	

SUPPLIES EXPENSE   ACCOUNT NO. 5050

Date		Explanation	Post Ref.	Debit	Credit	Balance Debit	Balance Credit

INSURANCE EXPENSE   ACCOUNT NO. 5060

Date		Explanation	Post Ref.	Debit	Credit	Balance Debit	Balance Credit
9/30	1X	Balance forward	✔			1 5 0 00	

POSTAGE EXPENSE   ACCOUNT NO. 5070

Date		Explanation	Post Ref.	Debit	Credit	Balance Debit	Balance Credit
9/30	1X	Balance forward	✔			5 0 00	

DEPRECIATION EXPENSE C.S. EQUIPMENT ACCOUNT NO. 5080

Date		Explanation	Post Ref.	Debit	Credit	Balance Debit	Balance Credit

DEPRECIATION EXPENSE OFFICE EQUIPMENT ACCOUNT NO. 5090

Date		Explanation	Post Ref.	Debit	Credit	Balance Debit	Balance Credit

SANCHEZ COMPUTER CENTER
POST-CLOSING TRIAL BALANCE
SEPTEMBER 30, 201X

	Dr.	Cr.

**MINI PRACTICE SET
SULLIVAN REALTY**

**SULLIVAN REALTY
GENERAL JOURNAL**

PAGE 1

Date	Account Titles and Description	PR	Dr.	Cr.

MINI PRACTICE SET
SULLIVAN REALTY

SULLIVAN REALTY
GENERAL JOURNAL

Date	Account Titles and Description	PR	Dr.	Cr.

MINI PRACTICE SET
SULLIVAN REALTY

SULLIVAN REALTY
GENERAL JOURNAL

PAGE 3

Date	Account Titles and Description	PR	Dr.	Cr.

MINI PRACTICE SET
SULLIVAN REALTY

SULLIVAN REALTY
GENERAL JOURNAL

PAGE 4

Date	Account Titles and Description	PR	Dr.	Cr.

MINI PRACTICE SET
SULLIVAN REALTY

SULLIVAN REALTY
GENERAL JOURNAL

PAGE 5

Date	Account Titles and Description	PR	Dr.	Cr.

MINI PRACTICE SET
SULLIVAN REALTY

SULLIVAN REALTY
GENERAL JOURNAL

PAGE 6

Date	Account Titles and Description	PR	Dr.	Cr.

MINI PRACTICE SET
SULLIVAN REALTY

MINI PRACTICE SET
SULLIVAN REALTY

CASH   ACCOUNT NO. 111

Date		Explanation	Post Ref.	Debit	Credit	Balance	
						Debit	Credit

MINI PRACTICE SET
SULLIVAN REALTY

ACCOUNTS RECEIVABLE   ACCOUNT NO. 112

Date	Explanation	Post Ref.	Debit	Credit	Balance Debit	Balance Credit

PREPAID RENT   ACCOUNT NO. 114

Date	Explanation	Post Ref.	Debit	Credit	Balance Debit	Balance Credit

OFFICE SUPPLIES   ACCOUNT NO. 115

Date	Explanation	Post Ref.	Debit	Credit	Balance Debit	Balance Credit

OFFICE EQUIPMENT   ACCOUNT NO. 121

Date	Explanation	Post Ref.	Debit	Credit	Balance Debit	Balance Credit

MINI PRACTICE SET: SULLIVAN REALTY

ACCUMULATED DEPRECIATION, OFFICE EQUIPMENT   ACCOUNT NO. 122

Date	Explanation	Post Ref.	Debit	Credit	Balance Debit	Balance Credit

AUTOMOBILE   ACCOUNT NO. 123

Date	Explanation	Post Ref.	Debit	Credit	Balance Debit	Balance Credit

ACCUMULATED DEPRECIATION, AUTOMOBILE   ACCOUNT NO. 124

Date	Explanation	Post Ref.	Debit	Credit	Balance Debit	Balance Credit

ACCOUNTS PAYABLE   ACCOUNT NO. 211

Date	Explanation	Post Ref.	Debit	Credit	Balance Debit	Balance Credit

SALARIES PAYABLE   ACCOUNT NO. 212

Date	Explanation	Post Ref.	Debit	Credit	Balance Debit	Balance Credit

MINI PRACTICE SET
SULLIVAN REALTY

JOHN SULLIVAN, CAPITAL   ACCOUNT NO. 311

Date	Explanation	Post Ref.	Debit	Credit	Balance Debit	Balance Credit

JOHN SULLIVAN, WITHDRAWALS   ACCOUNT NO. 312

Date	Explanation	Post Ref.	Debit	Credit	Balance Debit	Balance Credit

INCOME SUMMARY   ACCOUNT NO. 313

Date	Explanation	Post Ref.	Debit	Credit	Balance Debit	Balance Credit

MINI PRACTICE SET
SULLIVAN REALTY

COMMISSIONS EARNED   ACCOUNT NO. 411

Date	Explanation	Post Ref.	Debit	Credit	Balance Debit	Balance Credit

RENT EXPENSE   ACCOUNT NO. 511

Date	Explanation	Post Ref.	Debit	Credit	Balance Debit	Balance Credit

SALARIES EXPENSE   ACCOUNT NO. 512

Date	Explanation	Post Ref.	Debit	Credit	Balance Debit	Balance Credit

MINI PRACTICE SET
SULLIVAN REALTY

GAS EXPENSE   ACCOUNT NO. 513

Date		Explanation	Post Ref.	Debit	Credit	Balance	
						Debit	Credit

REPAIRS EXPENSE   ACCOUNT NO. 514

Date		Explanation	Post Ref.	Debit	Credit	Balance	
						Debit	Credit

TELEPHONE EXPENSE   ACCOUNT NO. 515

Date		Explanation	Post Ref.	Debit	Credit	Balance	
						Debit	Credit

ADVERTISING EXPENSE   ACCOUNT NO. 516

Date		Explanation	Post Ref.	Debit	Credit	Balance	
						Debit	Credit

MINI PRACTICE SET
SULLIVAN REALTY

OFFICE SUPPLIES EXPENSE   ACCOUNT NO. 517

Date	Explanation	Post Ref.	Debit	Credit	Balance Debit	Balance Credit

DEPRECIATION EXPENSE, OFFICE EQUIPMENT   ACCOUNT NO. 518

Date	Explanation	Post Ref.	Debit	Credit	Balance Debit	Balance Credit

DEPRECIATION EXPENSE, AUTOMOBILE   ACCOUNT NO. 519

Date	Explanation	Post Ref.	Debit	Credit	Balance Debit	Balance Credit

MISCELLANEOUS EXPENSE   ACCOUNT NO. 524

Date	Explanation	Post Ref.	Debit	Credit	Balance Debit	Balance Credit

MINI PRACTICE SET
SULLIVAN REALTY

Use the blank fold-out worksheets that accompanied your textbook.

SULLIVAN REALTY
INCOME STATEMENT
FOR MONTH ENDED JUNE 30, 201X

MINI PRACTICE SET
SULLIVAN REALTY

SULLIVAN REALTY
STATEMENT OF OWNER'S EQUITY
FOR MONTH ENDED JUNE 30, 201X

MINI PRACTICE SET
SULLIVAN REALTY

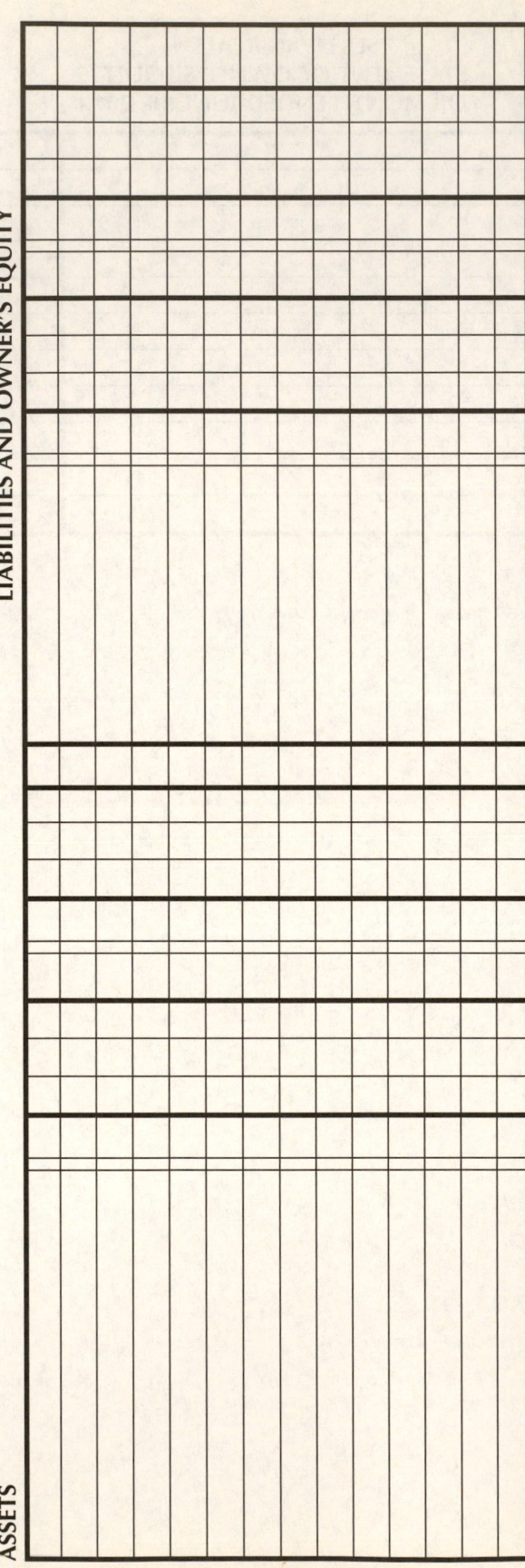

SULLIVAN REALTY
BALANCE SHEET
JUNE 30, 201X

LIABILITIES AND OWNER'S EQUITY

ASSETS

MINI PRACTICE SET
SULLIVAN REALTY

SULLIVAN REALTY
POST-CLOSING TRIAL BALANCE
JUNE 30, 201X

		Dr.		Cr.	

You can find the worksheet for July with the blank fold-out worksheets that accompanied your textbook.

MINI PRACTICE SET
SULLIVAN REALTY

SULLIVAN REALTY
INCOME STATEMENT
FOR MONTH ENDED JULY 31, 201X

MINI PRACTICE SET
SULLIVAN REALTY

SULLIVAN REALTY
STATEMENT OF OWNER'S EQUITY
FOR MONTH ENDED JULY 31, 201X

**MINI PRACTICE SET
SULLIVAN REALTY**

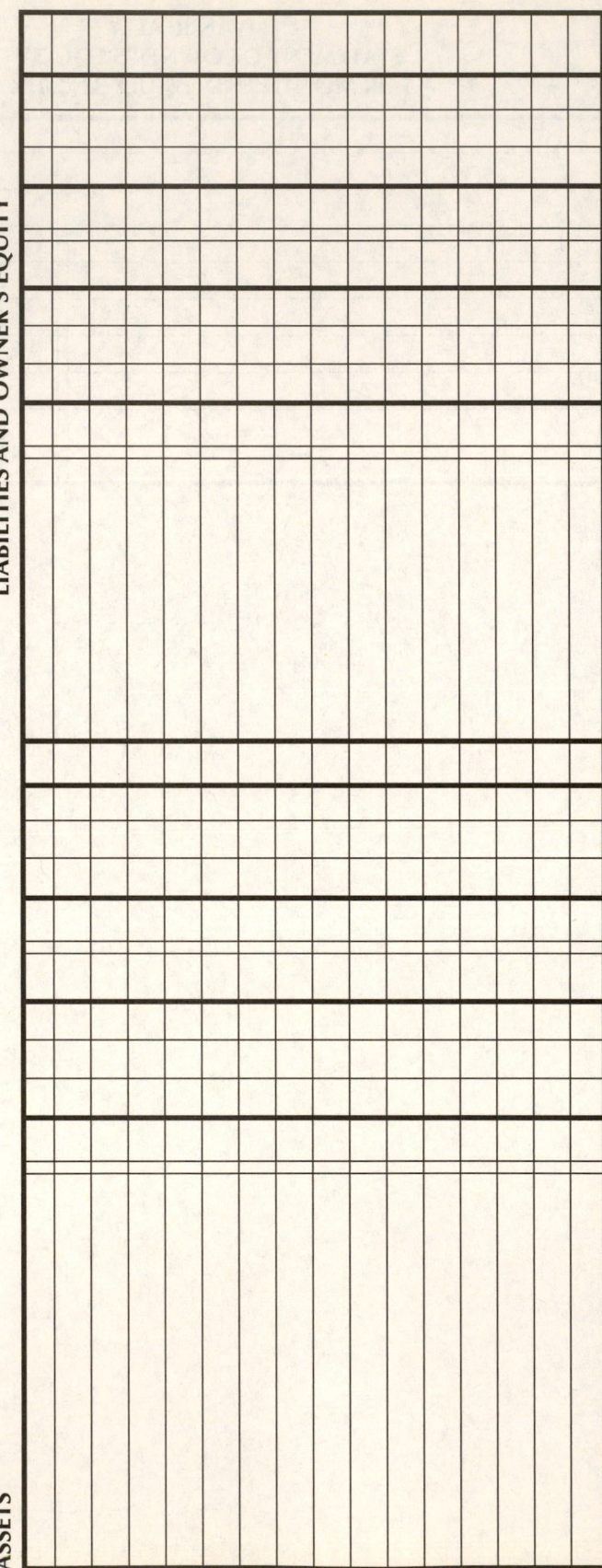

SULLIVAN REALTY
BALANCE SHEET
JULY 31, 201X

LIABILITIES AND OWNER'S EQUITY

ASSETS

MINI PRACTICE SET
SULLIVAN REALTY

SULLIVAN REALTY
POST-CLOSING TRIAL BALANCE
JULY 31, 201X

	Dr.	Cr.

BANKING PROCEDURES AND CONTROL OF CASH

6

INSTANT REPLAY: SELF-REVIEW QUIZ 6-1

Situation	Add to Bank Balance	Deduct from Bank Balance	Add to Checkbook Balance	Deduct from Checkbook Balance
1				
2				
3				
4				
5				
6				
7				
8				

INSTANT REPLAY: SELF-REVIEW QUIZ 6-2

PAGE 6

Date	Account Titles and Description	PR	Dr.	Cr.

AUXILIARY PETTY CASH RECORD

Date	Voucher No.	Description	Receipts	Payment	Category of Payment				
					Delivery Expense	General Expense	Account	Sundry Amount	

CHAPTER 6
CONCEPT CHECK

1.

A. _____ E. _____

B. _____ F. _____

C. _____

D. _____

2. _____ _____ _____ _____

3.

KING CO.
BANK RECONCILIATION
NOVEMBER 30, 201X

Checkbook	Bank

4.

A. _____ _____ _____ E. _____ _____ _____

B. _____ _____ _____ F. _____ _____ _____

C. _____ _____ _____

D. _____ _____ _____

5.

6.

FORMS FOR EXERCISES A OR B

6A-1 OR 6B-1

KING CO.
BANK RECONCILIATION AS OF MARCH 31, 201X

CHECKBOOK BALANCE

Ending Checkbook Balance	_____
Deduct:	_____
Bank Service Charge	_____
	_____
	_____
	_____
	_____
	_____
Reconciled Balance	_____

BALANCE PER BANK

Ending Bank Statement Balance	_____
Add:	_____
Deposit in Transit	_____
	_____
Deduct:	_____
Outstanding Checks	_____
	_____
Reconciled Balance	_____

6A-2 OR 6B-2

6A-3 OR 6B-3

EXERCISES (CONCLUDED)

6A-4 OR 6B-4

6A-5 OR 6B-5

    Beg. Change Fund
+Cash Register Total
=Cash should have on hand
– Counted Cash
= Cash Shortage

END OF CHAPTER PROBLEMS

PROBLEM 6A-1 OR PROBLEM 6B-1

SLACKS.COM
BANK RECONCILIATION AS OF JULY 31, 201X

BALANCE PER BANK

Bank Statement Balance

  Add: _____

Deduct: _____

              _____

Reconciled Balance _____

CHECKBOOK BALANCE

Checkbook Balance

  Add:

Deduct: _____

              _____

Reconciled Balance _____

PROBLEM 6A-1 OR PROBLEM 6B-1 (CONCLUDED)

Date		Account Titles and Description	PR	Dr.	Cr.

PROBLEM 6A-2 OR PROBLEM 6B-2

BOURNE NATIONAL BANK
RIO MEAN BRANCH
JIMMY'S DELI
8811 2ND ST.
BUGNA ,TEXAS   TELEPHONE 555-8311

This form is provided to help you balance your bank statement. If no errors are reported to auditors in ten days, the account will be considered correct.

Please notify us of any change in address.

Checks outstanding
(not charged to account)

Check No.	Amount
Total	

Sort the checks numerically or by date issued.
Check off on the stubs of your checkbook each check paid by bank.
List the numbers and amounts of checks still outstanding in the space provided at the left.
Verify the deposits in your checkbook with deposits credited on this statement. Bank balance show on this statement $_____

Plus: Deposits not
   credited on this statement $_____
      Subtotal $_____
Less: Checks outstanding $_____
Balance $_____

If your checkbook does not agree, enter any necessary adjustments:

_ _

_ _

_ _

Correct checkbook balance $_____

PROBLEM 6A-2 OR PROBLEM 6B-2 (CONCLUDED)

GENERAL JOURNAL

Date	Account Titles and Description	PR	Dr.	Cr.

PROBLEM 6A-3 OR PROBLEM 6B-3

JOYOUS CO.
GENERAL JOURNAL

Date		Account Titles and Description	PR	Dr.	Cr.

PROBLEM 6A-3 OR PROBLEM 6B-3 (CONCLUDED)

JOYOUS CO.
AUXILIARY PETTY CASH RECORD

Date	Voucher No.	Description	Receipts	Payment	Postage Expense	Office Supplies Expense	Account	Amount

Category of Payment — Postage Expense, Office Supplies Expense, Sundry (Account, Amount)

PROBLEM 6A-4 OR PROBLEM 6B-4

BURBANK CO.
GENERAL JOURNAL

PAGE 2

Date		Account Titles and Description	PR	Dr.	Cr.

PROBLEM 6A-4 OR PROBLEM 6B-4 (CONCLUDED)

BURBANK CO.
AUXILIARY PETTY CASH RECORD

Date	Voucher No.	Description	Receipts	Payment	Category of Payment				
					Postage Expense	Delivery Expense	Account	Sundry Amount	

CHAPTER 6
SUMMARY PRACTICE TEST
BANKING PROCEDURES AND CONTROL OF CASH

Part I Instructions

Fill in the blank(s) to complete the statement.

1. Online banking is _____ due to the internet.
2. Today, use of the _____ _____ has greatly increased.
3. All adjustments to the checkbook balance in the reconciliation process will require _____ _____.
4. Petty cash is a(n) _____ found on the balance sheet.
5. The auxiliary petty cash record is not a(n) _____.
6. A(n) _____ _____ is an asset used to make change for customer.
7. A cash overage will be _____ _____ on the income statement.
8. _____ _____ represents checks not processed by the bank at the time the bank statement was prepared.
9. When a bank credits your account, your balance will _____.
10. _____ is a procedure whereby the bank does not return the processed checks.

Part II Instructions

Indicate which of the following procedures are involved in each of the transactions below.

a. Recorded in General Journal
b. Recorded in both general journal and auxiliary petty cash record
c. Recorded only in auxiliary petty cash record
d. New check is written
e. Account petty cash is increased

1. EXAMPLE: Check issued to establish petty cash   b,d,e _____
2. Paid donation from petty cash   _____
3. Paid postage from petty cash   _____
4. Paid past purchases previously charged   _____
5. Paid for business luncheon with petty cash   _____
6. Issued check to pay for office supplies   _____
7. Replenished petty cash   _____
8. Paid local donation from petty cash   _____
9. Paid for past purchases bought on account   _____
10. Replenished petty cash   _____

Part III Instructions

Answer true or false to the following statements.

1. Online banking is decreasing today.
2. Petty cash is a liability found on the balance sheet.
3. Checks returned from the bank are placed in alphabetical order.
4. ATMs are being used less today than in the past.
5. Bank service charges represent an expense to the business.
6. The bank statement is the same as the bank reconciliation.
7. The balance in the company cash account will always equal the bank balance before the bank statement is received.
8. Deposit slips are needed in writing checks.
9. The signature must be presented when cashing a check.
10. The auxiliary petty cash record is posted monthly.
11. The petty cash account has a debit balance.
12. Replenishment of petty cash requires a new check.
13. The expenses paid from petty cash are journalized at time of replenishment.
14. Internal control only affects large companies.
15. A petty cash voucher records the expense into the ledger.
16. The petty cash fund must be replenished monthly.
17. The petty cash voucher identifies the account that will be charged.
18. The establishment of petty cash may require some judgment as to the amount of petty cash needed.
19. EFT is the same as safekeeping.
20. The drawer is the person who receives the check.
21. A debit memo will increase the depositor's balance.
22. A change fund uses only one denomination.
23. The payer is the person or company the check is payable to.

Part IV Instructions

Based on the following situation, prepare a bank reconciliation.

The checkbook balance of Logan Company is $5,263.08. The bank statement shows a bank balance of $7,980. The bank statement shows interest earned of $42 and a service charge of $29.76. There is a deposit in transit of $2,558.22. Outstanding checks total $3,762.90. The bank collected a note for Moore for $4,200. Moore Company forgot to deduct a check for $2,700 during the month.

SOLUTIONS TO SUMMARY PRACTICE TEST

Part I

1.	increasing	**6.**	change fund
2.	debit card	**7.**	miscellaneous income
3.	journal entries	**8.**	Checks outstanding
4.	asset	**9.**	increase
5.	journal	**10.**	Safekeeping

Part II

1.	b, d, e	**6.**	a, d
2.	c	**7.**	b, d
3.	c	**8.**	c
4.	a, d	**9.**	a, d
5.	c	**10.**	b, d

Part III

1.	false	**6.**	false	**11.**	true	**16.**	false	**21.**	false
2.	false	**7.**	false	**12.**	true	**17.**	true	**22.**	false
3.	false	**8.**	false	**13.**	true	**18.**	true	**23.**	false
4.	false	**9.**	true	**14.**	false	**19.**	false		
5.	true	**10.**	false	**15.**	false	**20.**	false		

Part IV

LOGAN CO.			BANK BALANCE	
Checkbook Balance		$5,263.08	Bank Balance	$7,980.00
ADD:			ADD:	
			Deposit	
Interest	$ 42		in Transit	2,558.22
Collection of note	4,200	4,242.00		$9,038.22
		8,005.08		
DEDUCT:			DEDUCT:	
Service Chg.	$ 29.76		Check outstanding	$3,762.90
Error	2,700.00	2,729.76		
Reconciled Balance		$6,775.32	Reconciled Balance	$6,775.32

CONTINUING PROBLEM—ON THE JOB FOR CHAPTER 6

SANCHEZ COMPUTER CENTER
GENERAL JOURNAL

PAGE 3

Date		Account Titles and Description	PR	Dr.				Cr.			

CASH   ACCOUNT NO. <u>1000</u>

Date		Explanation	Post Ref.	Debit	Credit	Balance Debit	Credit
9/30	1X	Balance forward	✔			1 6 4 5 00	

PETTY CASH   ACCOUNT NO. <u>1010</u>

Date		Explanation	Post Ref.	Debit	Credit	Balance Debit	Credit

ACCOUNTS RECEIVABLE   ACCOUNT NO. <u>1020</u>

Date		Explanation	Post Ref.	Debit	Credit	Balance		
							Debit	Credit
9/30	1X	Balance forward	✔			2 6 0 0 00	

PREPAID RENT   ACCOUNT NO. <u>1025</u>

Date		Explanation	Post Ref.	Debit	Credit	Balance		
							Debit	Credit
9/30	1X	Balance forward	✔			4 0 0 00	

SUPPLIES   ACCOUNT NO. <u>1030</u>

Date		Explanation	Post Ref.	Debit	Credit	Balance		
							Debit	Credit
9/30	1X	Balance forward	✔			9 0 00	

COMPUTER SHOP EQUIPMENT   ACCOUNT NO. <u>1080</u>

Date		Explanation	Post Ref.	Debit	Credit	Balance		
							Debit	Credit
9/30	1X	Balance forward	✔			2 4 0 0 00	

ACCUMULATED DEPRECIATION, COMPUTER SHOP EQUIPMENT   ACCOUNT NO. 1081

Date		Explanation	Post Ref.	Debit	Credit	Balance Debit	Balance Credit
9/30	1X	Balance forward	✔				9 9 00

OFFICE EQUIPMENT   ACCOUNT NO. 1090

Date		Explanation	Post Ref.	Debit	Credit	Balance Debit	Balance Credit
9/30	1X	Balance forward	✔			6 0 0 00	

ACCUMULATED DEPRECIATION, OFFICE EQUIPMENT   ACCOUNT NO. 1091

Date		Explanation	Post Ref.	Debit	Credit	Balance Debit	Balance Credit
9/30	1X	Balance forward	✔				2 0 00

ACCOUNTS PAYABLE   ACCOUNT NO. 2000

Date		Explanation	Post Ref.	Debit	Credit	Balance Debit	Balance Credit
9/30	1X	Balance forward	✔				2 1 0 00

T. FREEDMAN, CAPITAL ACCOUNT NO. 3000

Date		Explanation	Post Ref.	Debit	Credit	Balance Debit	Balance Credit
9/30	1X	Balance forward	✔				7 4 0 6 00

T. FREEDMAN, WITHDRAWALS ACCOUNT NO. 3010

Date		Explanation	Post Ref.	Debit	Credit	Balance Debit	Balance Credit

INCOME SUMMARY ACCOUNT NO. 3020

Date		Explanation	Post Ref.	Debit	Credit	Balance Debit	Balance Credit

SERVICE REVENUE   ACCOUNT NO. 4000

Date		Explanation	Post Ref.	Debit	Credit	Balance	
						Debit	Credit

ADVERTISING EXPENSE   ACCOUNT NO. 5010

Date		Explanation	Post Ref.	Debit	Credit	Balance	
						Debit	Credit

RENT EXPENSE   ACCOUNT NO. 5020

Date		Explanation	Post Ref.	Debit	Credit	Balance	
						Debit	Credit

UTILITIES EXPENSE — ACCOUNT NO. 5030

Date	Explanation	Post Ref.	Debit	Credit	Balance Debit	Balance Credit

PHONE EXPENSE — ACCOUNT NO. 5040

Date	Explanation	Post Ref.	Debit	Credit	Balance Debit	Balance Credit

SUPPLIES EXPENSE — ACCOUNT NO. 5050

Date	Explanation	Post Ref.	Debit	Credit	Balance Debit	Balance Credit

INSURANCE EXPENSE — ACCOUNT NO. 5060

Date	Explanation	Post Ref.	Debit	Credit	Balance Debit	Balance Credit

POSTAGE EXPENSE   ACCOUNT NO. <u>5070</u>

Date	Explanation	Post Ref.	Debit	Credit	Balance Debit	Balance Credit

DEPRECIATION EXPENSE, COMPUTER SHOP EQUIPMENT   ACCOUNT NO. <u>5080</u>

Date	Explanation	Post Ref.	Debit	Credit	Balance Debit	Balance Credit

DEPRECIATION EXPENSE, OFFICE EQUIPMENT   ACCOUNT NO. <u>5090</u>

Date	Explanation	Post Ref.	Debit	Credit	Balance Debit	Balance Credit

MISCELLANEOUS EXPENSE   ACCOUNT NO. <u>5100</u>

Date	Explanation	Post Ref.	Debit	Credit	Balance Debit	Balance Credit

SANCHEZ COMPUTER CENTER
TRIAL BALANCE
OCTOBER 31, 201X

AUXILIARY PETTY CASH RECORD

Date	Voucher No.	Description	Receipts	Payment	Category of Payment					
					Postage Expense	Supplies Expense	Supplies Account	Sundry Amount		

SANCHEZ COMPUTER CENTER
BANK RECONCILIATION AS OF SEPTEMBER 30, 201X

<u>**BALANCE PER BANK**</u>

Bank Statement Balance

  Add: _____

  Deduct: _____

_____

<u>**CHECKBOOK BALANCE**</u>

Checkbook Balance

  Add:

  Deduct: _____

_____

Reconciled Balance ====================

Reconciled Balance ====================

PAYROLL CONCEPTS AND PROCEDURES— EMPLOYEE TAXES

7

INSTANT REPLAY: SELF-REVIEW QUIZ 7-1

REGULAR EARNINGS

OVERTIME

GROSS EARNINGS

INSTANT REPLAY: SELF-REVIEW QUIZ 7-2

FIT

SIT

FICA - OASDI

FICA - Medicare

NET PAY

INSTANT REPLAY: SELF-REVIEW QUIZ 7-3

FICA - OASDI _____

FICA - Medicare _____

FUTA _____

SUTA _____

CHAPTER 7
CONCEPT CHECK

1. A. _____
_____
_____

B. _____
_____
_____

2. _____
_____
_____
_____
_____

3. _____
_____
_____
_____
_____
_____

4. A. _____ D. _____
B. _____ E. _____
C. _____ F. _____

5.

A. _____
B. _____
C. _____
D. _____

FORMS FOR EXERCISES A OR B

7A-1 OR 7B-1.

Mars _____

Valley _____

_____

Jones _____

_____

7A-2 OR 7B-2.

Zhu Rui   Tilla Palmer

_____   _____
_____   _____
_____   _____
_____   _____
_____   _____
_____   _____
_____   _____
_____   _____

7A-3 OR 7B-3.

_____
_____
_____
_____
_____

7A-4 OR 7B-4.

_____

_____
_____
_____
_____
_____

EXERCISES (CONCLUDED)

7A-5 OR 7B-5. _____
_____
_____
_____
_____

7A-6 OR 7B-6. _____
_____
_____
_____
_____

7A-7 OR 7B-7.

Employee	Weekly Pay	Weeks	Total	Taxable	Tax Rate	Tax

7A-8 OR 7B-8. _____
_____
_____

END OF CHAPTER PROBLEMS

PROBLEM 7A-1 OR PROBLEM 7B-1

Employee	Hourly Rate	# of Hours Worked	Gross Earnings
A.			
B.			
C.			
D.			

A.   B.

C.   D.

PROBLEM 7A-2 OR PROBLEM 7B-2

Use the fold-out payroll register that accompanied your textbook.

PROBLEM 7A-3 OR PROBLEM 7B-3

Use the fold-out payroll register that accompanied your textbook.

PROBLEM 7A-4 OR PROBLEM 7B-4

Use the fold-out payroll register that accompanied your textbook.

CHAPTER 7
SUMMARY PRACTICE TEST:
PAYROLL CONCEPTS AND PROCEDURES—EMPLOYEE TAXES

PART I INSTRUCTIONS

Fill in the blank(s) to complete the statement.

1. _____ _____ is gross pay less deductions.

2. Form _____ aids the employer in knowing how much to deduct for federal income tax.

3. The base for OASDI-Medicare will _____ _____ from year to year.

4. _____ _____ of the employer's tax guide has tables available for deductions for FIT and FICA (OASDI and Medicare).

5. _____ _____ _____ protects employees against losses due to injury or death incurred while on the job.

6. The two primary records used to keep track of payroll information are the _____ _____ and _____ _____ _____.

7. The employer is responsible for paying for_____.

8. _____ _____ is paid every two weeks.

9. A(n) _____ employee will only be paid for the hours actually worked.

10. An employer must pay FUTA on wages earned by each employee up to a maximum of $_____.

Part II Instructions

Answer true or false to the following.

1. OASDI is the tax form for SUTA.

2. Employers only pay FUTA and SUTA.

3. Employers pay a higher FICA-OASDI tax rate than employees do.

4. Gross pay plus deductions equals net pay.

5. Form W-4 aids in calculating FICA-OASDI.

6. The employer will match the employee's contribution for FICA (OASDI and Medicare).

7. The maximum tax credit for state unemployment tax is .8%.

8. A company may have different types of employees.

9. The Wage-Bracket Table makes it more difficult to calculate the amount of deductions for FIT.

10. A calendar year has no effect on taxes for FICA-Social Security.

Part III Instructions

Complete the chart below (use table in text as needed). Use the following information: Before this payroll Pete Bloom had earned $105,800. This week Pete earned $2,000 for the past two weeks. Assume an OASDI rate of Social Security of 6.2% up to $106,800. Medicare, 1.45%. FIT is $238.50. The state income tax is 7 percent.

GROSS PAY	TAXABLE FICA	DEDUCTIONS		FIT	SIT	NET PAY
		FICA				
		OASDI	Med.			

CHAPTER 7
SOLUTIONS TO SUMMARY PRACTICE TEST

Part I

1. Net Pay
2. W-4
3. not change
4. Circular E
5. Workers' Compensation Insurance

6. payroll register, employee earnings record
7. FUTA (SUTA)
8. Biweekly payroll
9. hourly
10. 7,000

Part II

1. false
2. false
3. false
4. false
5. false

6. true
7. false
8. true
9. false
10. false

Part III

OASDI	$1,000 x .062 =	$ 62.00	
Medicare	2,000 x .0145 =	29.00	
FIT		238.50	$2,000.00
SIT	2,000 x .07	140.00	– 469.50
Total deductions		$469.50	$1,530.50

CONTINUING PROBLEM—ON THE JOB FOR CHAPTER 7

(1)

SANCHEZ COMPUTER CENTER
GENERAL JOURNAL

PAGE 4

Date	Account Titles and Description	PR	Dr.	Cr.

SANCHEZ COMPUTER CENTER
GENERAL JOURNAL

Date		Account Titles and Description	PR	Dr.	Cr.

CASH   ACCOUNT NO. 1000

Date		Explanation	Post Ref.	Debit	Credit	Balance		
							Debit	Credit
10/31	1X	Balance forward	✔			4 2 9 3 00		

PETTY CASH   ACCOUNT NO. 1010

Date		Explanation	Post Ref.	Debit	Credit	Balance		
							Debit	Credit
10/31	1X	Balance forward	✔			1 0 0 00		

ACCOUNTS RECEIVABLE   ACCOUNT NO. 1020

Date		Explanation	Post Ref.	Debit	Credit	Balance		
							Debit	Credit
10/31	1X	Balance forward	✔			4 2 0 0 00		

PREPAID RENT   **ACCOUNT NO. 1025**

Date		Explanation	Post Ref.	Debit		Credit		Balance Debit		Balance Credit	
10/31	1X	Balance forward	✔					1 6 0 0 00			

SUPPLIES   **ACCOUNT NO. 1030**

Date		Explanation	Post Ref.	Debit		Credit		Balance Debit		Balance Credit	
10/31	1X	Balance forward	✔					9 0 00			

COMPUTER SHOP EQUIPMENT   **ACCOUNT NO. 1080**

Date		Explanation	Post Ref.	Debit		Credit		Balance Debit		Balance Credit	
10/31	1X	Balance forward	✔					2 4 0 0 00			

ACCUMULATED DEPRECIATION, COMPUTER SHOP EQUIPMENT   **ACCOUNT NO. 1081**

Date		Explanation	Post Ref.	Debit		Credit		Balance Debit		Balance Credit	
10/31	1X	Balance forward	✔							9 9 00	

OFFICE EQUIPMENT   ACCOUNT NO. <u>1090</u>

Date		Explanation	Post Ref.	Debit	Credit	Balance Debit	Balance Credit
10/31	1X	Balance forward	✔			6 0 0 00	

ACCUMULATED DEPRECIATION, OFFICE EQUIPMENT   ACCOUNT NO. <u>1091</u>

Date		Explanation	Post Ref.	Debit	Credit	Balance Debit	Balance Credit
10/31	1X	Balance forward	✔				2 0 00

ACCOUNTS PAYABLE   ACCOUNT NO. <u>2000</u>

Date		Explanation	Post Ref.	Debit	Credit	Balance Debit	Balance Credit
10/31	1X	Balance forward	✔				5 0 00

WAGES PAYABLE   ACCOUNT NO. <u>2010</u>

Date		Explanation	Post Ref.	Debit	Credit	Balance Debit	Balance Credit

FICA—OASDI PAYABLE   ACCOUNT NO. <u>2020</u>

Date		Explanation	Post Ref.	Debit	Credit	Balance	
						Debit	Credit

FICA—MEDICARE PAYABLE   ACCOUNT NO. <u>2030</u>

Date		Explanation	Post Ref.	Debit	Credit	Balance	
						Debit	Credit

FIT PAYABLE   ACCOUNT NO. <u>2040</u>

Date		Explanation	Post Ref.	Debit	Credit	Balance	
						Debit	Credit

SIT PAYABLE   ACCOUNT NO. <u>2050</u>

Date		Explanation	Post Ref.	Debit	Credit	Balance	
						Debit	Credit

T. FREEDMAN CAPITAL   ACCOUNT NO. 3000

Date		Explanation	Post Ref.	Debit	Credit	Balance	
						Debit	Credit
10/31	1X	Balance forward	✔				7 4 0 6 00

T. FREEDMAN WITHDRAWALS   ACCOUNT NO. 3010

Date		Explanation	Post Ref.	Debit	Credit	Balance	
						Debit	Credit
10/31	1X	Balance forward	✔			2 0 1 5 00	

SERVICE REVENUE   ACCOUNT NO. 4000

Date		Explanation	Post Ref.	Debit	Credit	Balance	
						Debit	Credit
10/31	1X	Balance forward	✔				7 8 0 0 00

ADVERTISING EXPENSE   ACCOUNT NO. 5010

Date		Explanation	Post Ref.	Debit	Credit	Balance	
						Debit	Credit

RENT EXPENSE   ACCOUNT NO. 5020

Date		Explanation	Post Ref.	Debit	Credit	Balance	
						Debit	Credit

UTILITIES EXPENSE   ACCOUNT NO. <u>5030</u>

Date		Explanation	Post Ref.	Debit	Credit	Balance Debit	Balance Credit

PHONE EXPENSE   ACCOUNT NO. <u>5040</u>

Date		Explanation	Post Ref.	Debit	Credit	Balance Debit	Balance Credit

SUPPLIES EXPENSE   ACCOUNT NO. <u>5050</u>

Date		Explanation	Post Ref.	Debit	Credit	Balance Debit	Balance Credit
10/31	1X		✔			4 2 00	

INSURANCE EXPENSE   ACCOUNT NO. <u>5060</u>

Date		Explanation	Post Ref.	Debit	Credit	Balance Debit	Balance Credit

POSTAGE EXPENSE   ACCOUNT NO. <u>5070</u>

Date		Explanation	Post Ref.	Debit	Credit	Balance Debit	Balance Credit
10/31	1X	Balance forward	✔			2 5 00	

DEPRECIATION EXPENSE C. S. EQUIPMENT   ACCOUNT NO. 5080

Date		Explanation	Post Ref.	Debit	Credit	Balance	
						Debit	Credit

DEPRECIATION EXPENSE OFFICE EQUIPMENT   ACCOUNT NO. 5090

Date		Explanation	Post Ref.	Debit	Credit	Balance	
						Debit	Credit

MISCELLANEOUS EXPENSE   ACCOUNT NO. 5100

Date		Explanation	Post Ref.	Debit	Credit	Balance	
						Debit	Credit
10/31	1X	Balance forward	✔			1 0 00	

WAGES EXPENSE   ACCOUNT NO. 5110

Date		Explanation	Post Ref.	Debit	Credit	Balance	
						Debit	Credit

(2) Use the fold-out payroll register that accompanied your textbook.

(3)

SANCHEZ COMPUTER CENTER
TRIAL BALANCE
NOVEMBER 30, 201X

		Dr.		Cr.	

THE EMPLOYER'S TAX RESPONSIBILITIES: PRINCIPLES AND PROCEDURES

INSTANT REPLAY: SELF-REVIEW QUIZ 8-1

GENERAL JOURNAL

PAGE 1

Date		Account Titles and Description	PR	Dr.			Cr.		

INSTANT REPLAY: SELF-REVIEW QUIZ 8-2

1.

2.

INSTANT REPLAY: SELF-REVIEW QUIZ 8-3

1. _____ 2. _____ 3. _____ 4. _____ 5. _____ 6. _____

CHAPTER 8

CONCEPT CHECK

1.

A.			
B.			
C.			
D.			
E.			

2.

A. _____

B. _____

C. _____

D. _____

3.

_____

_____

_____

_____

4.

A. _____

B. _____

C. _____

D. _____

E. _____

F. _____

G. _____

5.

A. _____

B. _____

C. _____

D. _____

E. _____

FORMS FOR EXERCISES A OR B

8A-1 OR 8B-1.

ACCOUNT	CATEGORY	DR/CR	STATEMENT FOUND ON

8A-2 OR 8B-2.

8A-3 OR 8B-3.

EXERCISES (CONCLUDED)

8A-4 OR 8B-4.

_____
_____
_____
_____
_____
_____
_____

8A-5 OR 8B-5.

_____
_____
_____
_____

8A-6 OR 8B-6.

_____
_____

8A-7 OR 8B-7.

_____
_____

8A-8 OR 8B-8.

END OF CHAPTER PROBLEMS

PROBLEM 8A-1 OR PROBLEM 8B-1

Employee	Allowance & Marital Status	Gross	FICA		Federal Income Tax
			OASDI	Medicare	

(2)

PROBLEM 8A-2 OR PROBLEM 8B-2

Date	Account Titles and Description	PR	Dr.	Cr.

PROBLEM 8A-2 OR PROBLEM 8B-2 (CONCLUDED)

Date		Account Titles and Description	PR	Dr.	Cr.

PROBLEM 8A-3 OR PROBLEM 8B-3

Form **941 for 201X:** Employer's QUARTERLY Federal Tax Return

(Rev. January 201X)   Department of the Treasury — Internal Revenue Service

950110

OMB No. 1545-0029

(EIN)
Employer identification number   ☐ ☐ – ☐ ☐ ☐ ☐ ☐ ☐ ☐

Name *(not your trade name)*

Trade name *(if any)*

Address

| Number | Street | | Suite or room number |

| City | | State | ZIP code |

Report for this Quarter of 2009
(Check one.)

☐ 1: January, February, March

☐ 2: April, May, June

☐ 3: July, August, September

☐ 4: October, November, December

Read the separate instructions before you complete Form 941. Type or print within the boxes.

Part 1: Answer these questions for this quarter.

1 Number of employees who received wages, tips, or other compensation for the pay period including: *Mar. 12* (Quarter 1), *June 12* (Quarter 2), *Sept. 12* (Quarter 3), *Dec. 12* (Quarter 4)   **1** ▢

2 Wages, tips, and other compensation . . . .   **2** ▢

3 Income tax withheld from wages, tips, and other compensation . . . . .   **3** ▢

4 If no wages, tips, and other compensation are subject to social security or Medicare tax   ☐ Check and go to line 6.

5 Taxable social security and Medicare wages and tips:

	Column 1		Column 2
5a Taxable social security wages	▢	× .124 =	▢
5b Taxable social security tips	▢	× .124 =	▢
5c Taxable Medicare wages & tips	▢	× .029 =	▢

5d Total social security and Medicare taxes (*Column 2,* lines 5a + 5b + 5c = line 5d) .   **5d** ▢

6 Total taxes before adjustments (lines 3 + 5d = line 6) . . . .   **6** ▢

7 **CURRENT QUARTER'S ADJUSTMENTS,** for example, a fractions of cents adjustment. See the instructions.

7a Current quarter's fractions of cents . . . .   ▢

7b Current quarter's sick pay . . . .   ▢

7c Current quarter's adjustments for tips and group-term life insurance   ▢

7d **TOTAL ADJUSTMENTS.** Combine all amounts on lines 7a through 7c . .   **7d** ▢

8 Total taxes after adjustments. Combine lines 6 and 7d . . . . . .   **8** ▢

9 Advance earned income credit (EIC) payments made to employees . . .   **9** ▢

10 Total taxes after adjustment for advance EIC (line 8 – line 9 = line 10) . . . . .   **10** ▢

11 Total deposits for this quarter, including overpayment applied from a prior quarter and overpayment applied from Form 941-X or Form 944-X . . . .   ▢

12a COBRA premium assistance payments (see instructions) . . . . .   ▢

12b Number of individuals provided COBRA premium assistance reported on line 12a . . . .   ▢

13 Add lines 11 and 12a . . . .   **13** ▢

14 **Balance due.** If line 10 is more than line 13, write the difference here   **14** ▢
For information on how to pay, see the instructions.

15 **Overpayment.** If line 13 is more than line 10, write the difference here   ▢   Check one ☐ Apply to next return. ☐ Send a refund.

▶ You **MUST** complete both pages of Form 941 and **SIGN** it.

Next ➡

For **Privacy Act and Paperwork Reduction Act Notice,** see the back of the Payment Voucher.   Cat. No. 17001Z   Form **941** (Rev. 1-201X)

Name _____ Class _____ Date _____

PROBLEM 8A-3 OR PROBLEM 8B-3 (CONCLUDED)

Name *(not your trade name)*	Employer identification number (EIN)

Part 2: Tell us about your deposit schedule and tax liability for this quarter.

If you are unsure about whether you are a monthly schedule depositor or a semiweekly schedule depositor, see *Pub. 15 (Circular E)*, section 11.

16 ☐☐ Write the state abbreviation for the state where you made your deposits OR write "MU" if you made your deposits in *multiple* states.

17 Check one: ☐ Line 10 is less than $2,500. Go to Part 3.

☐ You were a monthly schedule depositor for the entire quarter. Enter your tax liability for each month. Then go to Part 3.

Tax liability: Month 1 [·   ]

Month 2 [·   ]

Month 3 [·   ]

Total liability for quarter [·   ] Total must equal line 10.

☐ You were a semiweekly schedule depositor for any part of this quarter. Complete *Schedule B (Form 941): Report of Tax Liability for Semiweekly Schedule Depositors*, and attach it to Form 941.

Part 3: Tell us about your business. If a question does NOT apply to your business, leave it blank.

18 If your business has closed or you stopped paying wages . . . . ☐ Check here, and

enter the final date you paid wages [/   /   ] .

19 If you are a seasonal employer and you do not have to file a return for every quarter of the year . . ☐ Check here.

Part 4: May we speak with your third-party designee?

Do you want to allow an employee, a paid tax preparer, or another person to discuss this return with the IRS? See the instructions for details.

☐ Yes. Designee's name and phone number [   ] (   )   –

Select a 5-digit Personal Identification Number (PIN) to use when talking to the IRS. ☐☐☐☐☐

☐ No.

Part 5: Sign here. You MUST complete both pages of Form 941 and SIGN it.

Under penalties of perjury, I declare that I have examined this return, including accompanying schedules and statements, and to the best of my knowledge and belief, it is true, correct, and complete. Declaration of preparer (other than taxpayer) is based on all information of which preparer has any knowledge.

X Sign your name here [   ]

Print your name here [   ]

Print your title here [   ]

Date [/   /   ]

Best daytime phone (   )   –

Paid preparer's use only

Check if you are self-employed . . . . ☐

Preparer's name	[ ]	Preparer's SSN/PTIN	[ ]
Preparer's signature	[ ]	Date	[/ /]
Firm's name (or yours if self-employed)	[ ]	EIN	[ ]
Address	[ ]	Phone	( ) –
City	[ ] State [ ]	ZIP code	[ ]

Form **941** (Rev. 1-201X)

PROBLEM 8A-4 OR PROBLEM 8B-4

PROBLEM 8A-4 OR PROBLEM 8B-4 (CONTINUED)

Form **941 for 201X:** **Employer's QUARTERLY Federal Tax Return**

(Rev. January 201X)

Department of the Treasury — Internal Revenue Service

950110

OMB No. 1545-0029

(EIN)
Employer identification number ☐☐ – ☐☐☐☐☐☐☐

Name *(not your trade name)*

Trade name *(if any)*

Address
Number   Street   Suite or room number
City   State   ZIP code

Report for this Quarter of 2009
(Check one.)

☐ **1:** January, February, March

☐ **2:** April, May, June

☐ **3:** July, August, September

☐ **4:** October, November, December

Read the separate instructions before you complete Form 941. Type or print within the boxes.

Part 1: Answer these questions for this quarter.

1 Number of employees who received wages, tips, or other compensation for the pay period including: *Mar. 12* (Quarter 1), *June 12* (Quarter 2), *Sept. 12* (Quarter 3), *Dec. 12* (Quarter 4) **1** ☐

2 Wages, tips, and other compensation . . . . **2** ☐

3 Income tax withheld from wages, tips, and other compensation . . . . **3** ☐

4 If no wages, tips, and other compensation are subject to social security or Medicare tax ☐ Check and go to line 6.

5 Taxable social security and Medicare wages and tips:

	Column 1		Column 2
5a Taxable social security wages	☐	× .124 =	☐
5b Taxable social security tips	☐	× .124 =	☐
5c Taxable Medicare wages & tips	☐	× .029 =	☐

5d Total social security and Medicare taxes (*Column 2*, lines 5a + 5b + 5c = line 5d) . **5d** ☐

6 Total taxes before adjustments (lines 3 + 5d = line 6) . . . . **6** ☐

7 **CURRENT QUARTER'S ADJUSTMENTS,** for example, a fractions of cents adjustment. See the instructions.

7a Current quarter's fractions of cents . . . . ☐

7b Current quarter's sick pay . . . . ☐

7c Current quarter's adjustments for tips and group-term life insurance ☐

7d **TOTAL ADJUSTMENTS.** Combine all amounts on lines 7a through 7c . . . . . **7d** ☐

8 Total taxes after adjustments. Combine lines 6 and 7d . . . . **8** ☐

9 Advance earned income credit (EIC) payments made to employees . . . . . . **9** ☐

10 Total taxes after adjustment for advance EIC (line 8 – line 9 = line 10) . . . . . **10** ☐

11 Total deposits for this quarter, including overpayment applied from a prior quarter and overpayment applied from Form 941-X or Form 944-X . . . . ☐

12a COBRA premium assistance payments (see instructions) . . . . . ☐

12b Number of individuals provided COBRA premium assistance reported on line 12a . . . . . . ☐

13 Add lines 11 and 12a . . . . **13** ☐

14 **Balance due.** If line 10 is more than line 13, write the difference here . . . . . **14** ☐
For information on how to pay, see the instructions.

15 **Overpayment.** If line 13 is more than line 10, write the difference here ☐   Check one ☐ Apply to next return. ☐ Send a refund.

▶ You **MUST** complete both pages of Form 941 and **SIGN** it. Next ➡

For Privacy Act and Paperwork Reduction Act Notice, see the back of the Payment Voucher.   Cat. No. 17001Z   Form **941** (Rev. 1-201X)

PROBLEM 8A-4 OR PROBLEM 8B-4 (CONCLUDED)

950210

Name *(not your trade name)*	Employer identification number (EIN)

Part 2: Tell us about your deposit schedule and tax liability for this quarter.

If you are unsure about whether you are a monthly schedule depositor or a semiweekly schedule depositor, see *Pub. 15 (Circular E),* section 11.

16 ☐☐ Write the state abbreviation for the state where you made your deposits OR write "MU" if you made your deposits in *multiple* states.

17 Check one: ☐ Line 10 is less than $2,500. Go to Part 3.

☐ You were a monthly schedule depositor for the entire quarter. Enter your tax liability for each month. Then go to Part 3.

Tax liability: Month 1 [_____ . ___]

Month 2 [_____ . ___]

Month 3 [_____ . ___]

Total liability for quarter [_____ . ___] Total must equal line 10.

☐ You were a semiweekly schedule depositor for any part of this quarter. Complete *Schedule B (Form 941): Report of Tax Liability for Semiweekly Schedule Depositors,* and attach it to Form 941.

Part 3: Tell us about your business. If a question does NOT apply to your business, leave it blank.

18 If your business has closed or you stopped paying wages . . . . ☐ Check here, and

enter the final date you paid wages [/ /] .

19 If you are a seasonal employer and you do not have to file a return for every quarter of the year . ☐ Check here.

Part 4: May we speak with your third-party designee?

Do you want to allow an employee, a paid tax preparer, or another person to discuss this return with the IRS? See the instructions for details.

☐ Yes. Designee's name and phone number [_____] (___) ___ – ____

Select a 5-digit Personal Identification Number (PIN) to use when talking to the IRS. ☐☐☐☐☐

☐ No.

Part 5: Sign here. You MUST complete both pages of Form 941 and SIGN it.

Under penalties of perjury, I declare that I have examined this return, including accompanying schedules and statements, and to the best of my knowledge and belief, it is true, correct, and complete. Declaration of preparer (other than taxpayer) is based on all information of which preparer has any knowledge.

X Sign your name here [_____]

Print your name here [_____]

Print your title here [_____]

Date [/ /]

Best daytime phone (___) ___ – ____

Paid preparer's use only   Check if you are self-employed . . . . ☐

Preparer's name	[_____]	Preparer's SSN/PTIN	[_____]
Preparer's signature	[_____]	Date	[/ /]
Firm's name (or yours if self-employed)	[_____]	EIN	[_____]
Address	[_____]	Phone	(___) ___ – ____
City	[_____] State [____]	ZIP code	[_____]

PROBLEM 8A-5 OR PROBLEM 8B-5

Continuing Problem for Chapter 8- Sanchez Computer Center

Form **940 for 201X:** Employer's Annual Federal Unemployment (FUTA) Tax Return

Department of the Treasury — Internal Revenue Service

850110

OMB No. 1545-0028

(EIN)
Employer identification number ☐☐ – ☐☐☐☐☐☐☐

Name *(not your trade name)* _____

Trade name *(if any)* _____

Address _____

Number   Street   Suite or room number

City   State   ZIP code

Type of Return
(Check all that apply.)

☐ **a.** Amended

☐ **b.** Successor employer

☐ **c.** No payments to employees in 2010

☐ **d.** Final: Business closed or stopped paying wages

Read the separate instructions before you fill out this form. Please type or print within the boxes.

Part 1: Tell us about your return. If any line does NOT apply, leave it blank.

1 If you were required to pay your state unemployment tax in ...

   1a One state only, write the state abbreviation . . . . **1a** ☐☐

   - OR -

   1b More than one state (You are a multi-state employer) . . . . **1b** ☐ Check here. Fill out Schedule A.

2 If you paid wages in a state that is subject to **CREDIT REDUCTION** . . . . **2** ☐ Check here. Fill out Schedule A (Form 940), Part 2.

Part 2: Determine your FUTA tax before adjustments for 2010. If any line does NOT apply, leave it blank.

3 Total payments to all employees . . . . **3** ☐

4 Payments exempt from FUTA tax . . . . . . **4** ☐

   Check all that apply: **4a** ☐ Fringe benefits **4c** ☐ Retirement/Pension **4e** ☐ Other

   4b ☐ Group-term life insurance **4d** ☐ Dependent care

5 Total of payments made to each employee in excess of $7,000 . . . . **5** ☐

6 Subtotal (line 4 + line 5 = line 6) . . . . **6** ☐

7 Total taxable FUTA wages (line 3 – line 6 = line 7) . . . . **7** ☐

8 FUTA tax before adjustments (line 7 × .008 = line 8) . . . . . **8** ☐

Part 3: Determine your adjustments. If any line does NOT apply, leave it blank.

9 If ALL of the taxable FUTA wages you paid were excluded from state unemployment tax, multiply line 7 by .054 (line 7 × .054 = line 9). Then go to line 12 . . . . . . **9** ☐

10 If SOME of the taxable FUTA wages you paid were excluded from state unemployment tax, OR you paid ANY state unemployment tax late (after the due date for filing Form 940), fill out the worksheet in the instructions. Enter the amount from line 7 of the worksheet . . . . . **10** ☐

11 If credit reduction applies, enter the amount from line 3 of Schedule A (Form 940) . . . . . **11** ☐

Part 4: Determine your FUTA tax and balance due or overpayment for 2010. If any line does NOT apply, leave it blank.

12 Total FUTA tax after adjustments (lines 8 + 9 + 10 + 11 = line 12) . . . . **12** ☐

13 FUTA tax deposited for the year, including any overpayment applied from a prior year **13** ☐

14 Balance due (If line 12 is more than line 13, enter the difference on line 14.)

   • If line 14 is more than $500, you must deposit your tax.

   • If line 14 is $500 or less, you may pay with this return. For more information on how to pay, see the separate instructions **14** ☐

15 Overpayment (If line 13 is more than line 12, enter the difference on line 15 and check a box below.) . . . . **15** ☐

Check one: ☐ Apply to next return.
         ☐ Send a refund.

▶ You **MUST** fill out both pages of this form and **SIGN** it.

Next ▶

For Privacy Act and Paperwork Reduction Act Notice, see the back of Form 940-V, Payment Voucher.

Cat. No. 11234O

Form **940** (201X)

PROBLEM 8A-5 OR PROBLEM 8B-5 (CONCLUDED)

Continuing Problem for Chapter 8- Sanchez Computer Center (Continued)

850210

Name (not your trade name)	Employer identification number (EIN)

Part 5: Report your FUTA tax liability by quarter only if line 12 is more than $500. If not, go to Part 6.

16 Report the amount of your FUTA tax liability for each quarter; do NOT enter the amount you deposited. If you had no liability for a quarter, leave the line blank.

16a **1st quarter** (January 1 – March 31)	16a	.
16b **2nd quarter** (April 1 – June 30)	16b	.
16c **3rd quarter** (July 1 – September 30)	16c	.
16d **4th quarter** (October 1 – December 31)	16d	.

17 **Total tax liability for the year** (lines 16a + 16b + 16c + 16d = line 17) 17   .   **Total must equal line 12.**

Part 6: May we speak with your third-party designee?

Do you want to allow an employee, a paid tax preparer, or another person to discuss this return with the IRS? See the instructions for details.

☐ **Yes.** Designee's name and phone number

Select a 5-digit Personal Identification Number (PIN) to use when talking to IRS

☐ **No.**

Part 7: Sign here. You MUST fill out both pages of this form and SIGN it.

Under penalties of perjury, I declare that I have examined this return, including accompanying schedules and statements, and to the best of my knowledge and belief, it is true, correct, and complete, and that no part of any payment made to a state unemployment fund claimed as a credit was, or is to be, deducted from the payments made to employees. Declaration of preparer (other than taxpayer) is based on all information of which preparer has any knowledge.

✗ **Sign your name here**

Print your name here

Print your title here

Date   /   /

Best daytime phone

Paid preparer use only   Check if you are self-employed . . . . ☐

Preparer's name		PTIN	
Preparer's signature		Date	/ /
Firm's name (or yours if self-employed)		EIN	
Address		Phone	
City	State	ZIP code	

Page **2**   Form **940** (201X)

CHAPTER 8
SUMMARY PRACTICE TEST:
THE EMPLOYER'S TAX RESPONSIBILITIES:
PRINCIPLES AND PROCEDURES

Part I Instructions

Fill in the blank(s) to complete the statement.

1. Form 941 is completed _____.
2. The payroll tax expense for the employer is made up of _____, _____, and FUTA.
3. Data from the _____ _____ will provide the needed information to record the payroll in the general journal.
4. SUTA is usually paid _____.
5. FUTA Payable is a _____ found on the _____ _____.
6. Form 941 summarizes the taxes owed for _____ and _____.
7. _____ _____ _____ will tell if a deposit is to be made monthly or semiweekly for FIT and Social Security.
8. Form _____ is prepared quarterly to summarize tax liabilities for FICA (Social Security and Medicare) and FIT.
9. The _____ _____ _____ _____ is required to be given to employees by January 31 following the year employed.
10. _____ does not have a merit rating like SUTA.

Part II Instructions

Answer true or false to the following.

1. Prepaid Workers' Compensation Insurance is a liability.
2. Payroll taxes are recorded as assets for a business.
3. Payroll Tax Expense is made up of FICA, SUTA, and FIT.
4. Frequency of deposits relating to Form 941 is based on amount of tax liability in look-back periods.
5. The normal balance of FIT payable is a debit.
6. The individual earnings record provides the data to prepare W-2s.
7. A tax calendar provides little help to the employer involving the payment of tax liabilities.
8. Form 941 is completed twice a year.
9. A year-end adjusting entry is needed for workers' compensation.
10. Form 8109 relates only to Form 940.

Part III Instructions

Complete the following table:

ACCOUNT	CATEGORY	FOUND ON WHICH REPORT
1. Salaries Payable		
2. FUTA Payable		
3. SUTA Payable		
4. OASDI Tax Payable—Medicare		
5. FIT Payable		
6. Office Salaries Expense		

Part IV Instructions

Complete the following table:

	4 QUARTERS LOOK-BACK PERIOD LIABILITY	PAYROLL PAID WEEKLY	TAX PAID BY:
Sit. A	$40,000	October	?
Sit. B	75,000		
		on Wed.	?
		on Thurs.	?
		on Fri.	?
		on Sat.	?
		on Sun.	?
		on Mon.	?
		on Tues.	?

Why is the depositor in situation A classified as a monthly depositor while in situation B the depositor is classified as semiweekly?

SOLUTIONS TO SUMMARY PRACTICE TEST

Part I

1. quarterly
2. FICA (OASDI and Medicare), SUTA
3. payroll register
4. quarterly
5. liability, balance sheet
6. FICA (OASDI and Medicare), FIT
7. Look-back periods
8. 941
9. Wage and Tax Statement
10. FUTA

Part II

1. false
2. false
3. false
4. true
5. false
6. true
7. false
8. false
9. true
10. false

Part III

1. Liability; Balance Sheet
2. Liability; Balance Sheet
3. Liability; Balance Sheet
4. Liability; Balance Sheet
5. Liability; Balance Sheet
6. Expense; Income Statement

Part IV

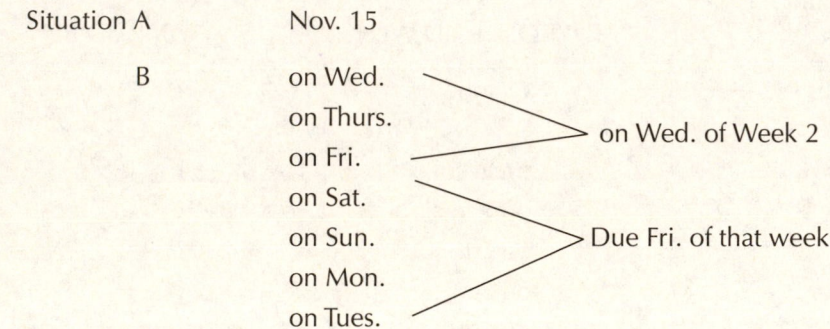

Situation A   Nov. 15

The depositor in situation A is classified as a monthly depositor because its tax liability of $40,000 during the look-back period was less than the $50,000 limit.

On the other hand, the depositor in situation B owed $75,000 during the look-back period. Since this is greater than the $50,000 limit, it was classified as a semiweekly depositor.

Name _____ Class _____ Date _____

CONTINUING PROBLEM—ON THE JOB FOR CHAPTER 8
SANCHEZ COMPUTER CENTER

SANCHEZ COMPUTER CENTER
GENERAL JOURNAL

PAGE 5

Date	Account Titles and Description	PR	Dr.	Cr.

CONTINUING PROBLEM FOR CHAPTER 8
SANCHEZ COMPUTER CENTER

SANCHEZ COMPUTER CENTER
GENERAL JOURNAL

PAGE 6

Date		Account Titles and Description	PR	Dr.	Cr.

Name _____ Class _____ Date _____

CONTINUING PROBLEM FOR CHAPTER 8
SANCHEZ COMPUTER CENTER

Mini Practice Set

Form **941 for 201X:** Employer's QUARTERLY Federal Tax Return

(Rev. January 201X) Department of the Treasury — Internal Revenue Service

950110

OMB No. 1545-0029

(EIN)
Employer identification number ☐☐ – ☐☐☐☐☐☐☐

Name *(not your trade name)*

Trade name *(if any)*

Address
Number   Street   Suite or room number
City   State   ZIP code

Report for this Quarter of 2009
(Check one.)

☐ **1:** January, February, March
☐ **2:** April, May, June
☐ **3:** July, August, September
☐ **4:** October, November, December

Read the separate instructions before you complete Form 941. Type or print within the boxes.

Part 1: Answer these questions for this quarter.

1 Number of employees who received wages, tips, or other compensation for the pay period including: *Mar. 12* (Quarter 1), *June 12* (Quarter 2), *Sept. 12* (Quarter 3), *Dec. 12* (Quarter 4) **1** ☐

2 Wages, tips, and other compensation . . . . **2** ☐.

3 Income tax withheld from wages, tips, and other compensation . . . . **3** ☐.

4 If no wages, tips, and other compensation are subject to social security or Medicare tax ☐ Check and go to line 6.

5 Taxable social security and Medicare wages and tips:

	Column 1		Column 2
5a Taxable social security wages	☐.	× .124 =	☐.
5b Taxable social security tips	☐.	× .124 =	☐.
5c Taxable Medicare wages & tips	☐.	× .029 =	☐.

5d Total social security and Medicare taxes (*Column 2,* lines 5a + 5b + 5c = line 5d) . **5d** ☐.

6 Total taxes before adjustments (lines 3 + 5d = line 6) . . . . **6** ☐.

7 **CURRENT QUARTER'S ADJUSTMENTS,** for example, a fractions of cents adjustment. See the instructions.

7a Current quarter's fractions of cents . . . . . . ☐.

7b Current quarter's sick pay . . . . . . ☐.

7c Current quarter's adjustments for tips and group-term life insurance ☐.

7d **TOTAL ADJUSTMENTS.** Combine all amounts on lines 7a through 7c . . . **7d** ☐.

8 Total taxes after adjustments. Combine lines 6 and 7d . . . . . **8** ☐.

9 Advance earned income credit (EIC) payments made to employees . . . . . . **9** ☐.

10 Total taxes after adjustment for advance EIC (line 8 – line 9 = line 10) . . . . **10** ☐.

11 Total deposits for this quarter, including overpayment applied from a prior quarter and overpayment applied from Form 941-X or Form 944-X . ☐.

12a **COBRA** premium assistance payments (see instructions) . . . . . ☐.

12b Number of individuals provided COBRA premium assistance reported on line 12a . ☐

13 Add lines 11 and 12a . . . . **13** ☐.

14 **Balance due.** If line 10 is more than line 13, write the difference here . . . . **14** ☐.
For information on how to pay, see the instructions.

15 **Overpayment.** If line 13 is more than line 10, write the difference here ☐. ☐ Apply to next return.
Check one ☐ Send a refund.

▶ You **MUST** complete both pages of Form 941 and **SIGN** it. Next ➡

For Privacy Act and Paperwork Reduction Act Notice, see the back of the Payment Voucher. Cat. No. 17001Z Form **941** (Rev. 1-201X)

CONTINUING PROBLEM FOR CHAPTER 8
SANCHEZ COMPUTER CENTER
Mini Practice Set (Continued)

9502010

Name *(not your trade name)*	Employer identification number (EIN)

Part 2: Tell us about your deposit schedule and tax liability for this quarter.

If you are unsure about whether you are a monthly schedule depositor or a semiweekly schedule depositor, see *Pub. 15 (Circular E),* section 11.

16 ☐☐ Write the state abbreviation for the state where you made your deposits OR write "MU" if you made your deposits in *multiple* states.

17 Check one: ☐ Line 10 is less than $2,500. Go to Part 3.

☐ You were a monthly schedule depositor for the entire quarter. Enter your tax liability for each month. Then go to Part 3.

Tax liability: Month 1 [.]

Month 2 [.]

Month 3 [.]

Total liability for quarter [.] Total must equal line 10.

☐ You were a semiweekly schedule depositor for any part of this quarter. Complete *Schedule B (Form 941): Report of Tax Liability for Semiweekly Schedule Depositors,* and attach it to Form 941.

Part 3: Tell us about your business. If a question does NOT apply to your business, leave it blank.

18 If your business has closed or you stopped paying wages . . . . ☐ Check here, and

enter the final date you paid wages [/   /   ] .

19 If you are a seasonal employer and you do not have to file a return for every quarter of the year . . ☐ Check here.

Part 4: May we speak with your third-party designee?

Do you want to allow an employee, a paid tax preparer, or another person to discuss this return with the IRS? See the instructions for details.

☐ Yes. Designee's name and phone number [   ] (____) ____ – ____

Select a 5-digit Personal Identification Number (PIN) to use when talking to the IRS. ☐ ☐ ☐ ☐ ☐

☐ No.

Part 5: Sign here. You MUST complete both pages of Form 941 and SIGN it.

Under penalties of perjury, I declare that I have examined this return, including accompanying schedules and statements, and to the best of my knowledge and belief, it is true, correct, and complete. Declaration of preparer (other than taxpayer) is based on all information of which preparer has any knowledge.

X Sign your name here [   ]

Print your name here [   ]

Print your title here [   ]

Date [/   /   ]

Best daytime phone (____) ____ – ____

Paid preparer's use only   Check if you are self-employed . . . . ☐

Preparer's name	[ ]	Preparer's SSN/PTIN	[ ]
Preparer's signature	[ ]	Date	[/ /]
Firm's name (or yours if self-employed)	[ ]	EIN	[ ]
Address	[ ]	Phone	(____) ____ – ____
City	[ ] State [ ]	ZIP code	[ ]

Continuing Problem for Chapter 8- Sanchez Computer Center

Form **940 for 201X:** Employer's Annual Federal Unemployment (FUTA) Tax Return   850110

Department of the Treasury — Internal Revenue Service

OMB No. 1545-0028

(EIN)
Employer identification number ☐☐ - ☐☐☐☐☐☐☐

Name (not your trade name) _____

Trade name (if any) _____

Address _____
Number   Street   Suite or room number
_____
City   State   ZIP code

Type of Return
(Check all that apply.)

☐ **a.** Amended
☐ **b.** Successor employer
☐ **c.** No payments to employees in 2010
☐ **d.** Final: Business closed or stopped paying wages

Read the separate instructions before you fill out this form. Please type or print within the boxes.

Part 1: Tell us about your return. If any line does NOT apply, leave it blank.

1   If you were required to pay your state unemployment tax in ...

    1a **One state only,** write the state abbreviation . . . . . **1a** ☐☐
    - OR -
    1b **More than one state** (You are a multi-state employer) . . . . **1b** ☐ Check here. Fill out Schedule A.

2   If you paid wages in a state that is subject to **CREDIT REDUCTION** . . . . **2** ☐ Check here. Fill out Schedule A (Form 940), Part 2.

Part 2: Determine your FUTA tax before adjustments for 2010. If any line does NOT apply, leave it blank.

3   Total payments to all employees . . . . **3** ☐ .

4   Payments exempt from FUTA tax . . . . **4** ☐ .

    Check all that apply: **4a** ☐ Fringe benefits **4c** ☐ Retirement/Pension **4e** ☐ Other
    4b ☐ Group-term life insurance **4d** ☐ Dependent care

5   Total of payments made to each employee in excess of $7,000 . . . . . . **5** ☐ .

6   **Subtotal** (line 4 + line 5 = line 6) . . . . **6** ☐ .

7   **Total taxable FUTA wages** (line 3 – line 6 = line 7) . . . . **7** ☐ .

8   **FUTA tax before adjustments** (line 7 × .008 = line 8) . . . . . **8** ☐ .

Part 3: Determine your adjustments. If any line does NOT apply, leave it blank.

9   If ALL of the taxable FUTA wages you paid were excluded from state unemployment tax, multiply line 7 by **.054** (line 7 × .054 = line 9). Then go to line 12 . . . . . **9** ☐ .

10   If SOME of the taxable FUTA wages you paid were excluded from state unemployment tax, OR you paid ANY state unemployment tax late (after the due date for filing Form 940), fill out the worksheet in the instructions. Enter the amount from line 7 of the worksheet . . . . . **10** ☐ .

11   If credit reduction applies, enter the amount from line 3 of Schedule A (Form 940) . . . . . **11** ☐ .

Part 4: Determine your FUTA tax and balance due or overpayment for 2010. If any line does NOT apply, leave it blank.

12   Total FUTA tax after adjustments (lines 8 + 9 + 10 + 11 = line 12) . . . . **12** ☐ .

13   FUTA tax deposited for the year, including any overpayment applied from a prior year . **13** ☐ .

14   Balance due (If line 12 is more than line 13, enter the difference on line 14.)
    • If line 14 is more than $500, you must deposit your tax.
    • If line 14 is $500 or less, you may pay with this return. For more information on how to pay, see the separate instructions . . . . . **14** ☐ .

15   Overpayment (If line 13 is more than line 12, enter the difference on line 15 and check a box below.) . . . . **15** ☐ .

Check one: ☐ Apply to next return.
    ☐ Send a refund.

▶ You **MUST** fill out both pages of this form and **SIGN** it.

Next ▶

For Privacy Act and Paperwork Reduction Act Notice, see the back of Form 940-V, Payment Voucher.   Cat. No. 112340   Form **940** (201X)

Continuing Problem for Chapter 8- Sanchez Computer Center (Continued)

850210

| Name (not your trade name) | Employer identification number (EIN) |

Part 5: Report your FUTA tax liability by quarter only if line 12 is more than $500. If not, go to Part 6.

16 Report the amount of your FUTA tax liability for each quarter; do NOT enter the amount you deposited. If you had no liability for a quarter, leave the line blank.

16a **1st quarter** (January 1 – March 31) . . . . 16a [.]

16b **2nd quarter** (April 1 – June 30) . . . . 16b [.]

16c **3rd quarter** (July 1 – September 30) . . . . 16c [.]

16d **4th quarter** (October 1 – December 31) . . . . 16d [.]

17 **Total tax liability for the year** (lines 16a + 16b + 16c + 16d = line 17) 17 [.] **Total must equal line 12.**

Part 6: May we speak with your third-party designee?

Do you want to allow an employee, a paid tax preparer, or another person to discuss this return with the IRS? See the instructions for details.

☐ **Yes.** Designee's name and phone number [_____] [_____]

Select a 5-digit Personal Identification Number (PIN) to use when talking to IRS [ ][ ][ ][ ][ ]

☐ **No.**

Part 7: Sign here. You MUST fill out both pages of this form and SIGN it.

Under penalties of perjury, I declare that I have examined this return, including accompanying schedules and statements, and to the best of my knowledge and belief, it is true, correct, and complete, and that no part of any payment made to a state unemployment fund claimed as a credit was, or is to be, deducted from the payments made to employees. Declaration of preparer (other than taxpayer) is based on all information of which preparer has any knowledge.

✗ **Sign your name here** [_____]

Print your name here [_____]

Print your title here [_____]

Date [/ /]

Best daytime phone [_____]

Paid preparer use only Check if you are self-employed . . . ☐

Preparer's name	[_____]	PTIN	[_____]
Preparer's signature	[_____]	Date	[/ /]
Firm's name (or yours if self-employed)	[_____]	EIN	[_____]
Address	[_____]	Phone	[_____]
City	[_____]	State [____]	ZIP code	[_____]

Mini Practice Set

Form **941 for 201X:** **Employer's QUARTERLY Federal Tax Return**

(Rev. January 201X)

Department of the Treasury — Internal Revenue Service

950110

OMB No. 1545-0029

(EIN)
Employer identification number ☐☐ – ☐☐☐☐☐☐☐

Name (not your trade name) _____

Trade name (if any) _____

Address _____
Number   Street   Suite or room number
_____
City   State   ZIP code

Report for this Quarter of 2009
(Check one.)

☐ **1:** January, February, March

☐ **2:** April, May, June

☐ **3:** July, August, September

☐ **4:** October, November, December

Read the separate instructions before you complete Form 941. Type or print within the boxes.

Part 1: Answer these questions for this quarter.

1 Number of employees who received wages, tips, or other compensation for the pay period
including: *Mar. 12* (Quarter 1), *June 12* (Quarter 2), *Sept. 12* (Quarter 3), *Dec. 12* (Quarter 4) **1** _____

2 Wages, tips, and other compensation . . . . **2** _____

3 Income tax withheld from wages, tips, and other compensation . . . . **3** _____

4 If no wages, tips, and other compensation are subject to social security or Medicare tax ☐ Check and go to line 6.

5 Taxable social security and Medicare wages and tips:

	Column 1		Column 2
5a Taxable social security wages	_____	× .124 =	_____
5b Taxable social security tips	_____	× .124 =	_____
5c Taxable Medicare wages & tips	_____	× .029 =	_____

5d Total social security and Medicare taxes (*Column 2,* lines 5a + 5b + 5c = line 5d) . **5d** _____

6 Total taxes before adjustments (lines 3 + 5d = line 6) . . . . **6** _____

7 **CURRENT QUARTER'S ADJUSTMENTS,** for example, a fractions of cents adjustment.
See the instructions.

7a Current quarter's fractions of cents . . . . _____

7b Current quarter's sick pay . . . . _____

7c Current quarter's adjustments for tips and group-term life insurance _____

7d **TOTAL ADJUSTMENTS.** Combine all amounts on lines 7a through 7c . . . **7d** _____

8 Total taxes after adjustments. Combine lines 6 and 7d . . . . . . **8** _____

9 Advance earned income credit (EIC) payments made to employees . . . . **9** _____

10 Total taxes after adjustment for advance EIC (line 8 – line 9 = line 10) . . . . **10** _____

11 Total deposits for this quarter, including overpayment applied from a
prior quarter and overpayment applied from Form 941-X or
Form 944-X . . . . _____

12a COBRA premium assistance payments (see instructions) . . . . . _____

12b Number of individuals provided COBRA premium
assistance reported on line 12a . . . . _____

13 Add lines 11 and 12a . . . . **13** _____

14 Balance due. If line 10 is more than line 13, write the difference here . . . . **14** _____
For information on how to pay, see the instructions. ☐ Apply to next return.

15 Overpayment. If line 13 is more than line 10, write the difference here _____ Check one ☐ Send a refund.

▶ You **MUST** complete both pages of Form 941 and **SIGN** it. Next ➡

For Privacy Act and Paperwork Reduction Act Notice, see the back of the Payment Voucher. Cat. No. 17001Z Form **941** (Rev. 1-201X)

Mini Practice Set (Continued)

9502010

Name (not your trade name)	**Employer identification number (EIN)**

Part 2: Tell us about your deposit schedule and tax liability for this quarter.

If you are unsure about whether you are a monthly schedule depositor or a semiweekly schedule depositor, see *Pub. 15 (Circular E)*, section 11.

16 ☐☐ Write the state abbreviation for the state where you made your deposits OR write "MU" if you made your deposits in *multiple* states.

17 Check one: ☐ Line 10 is less than $2,500. Go to Part 3.

☐ You were a monthly schedule depositor for the entire quarter. Enter your tax liability for each month. Then go to Part 3.

Tax liability: Month 1 [.   ]

Month 2 [.   ]

Month 3 [.   ]

Total liability for quarter [.   ] Total must equal line 10.

☐ You were a semiweekly schedule depositor for any part of this quarter. Complete *Schedule B (Form 941): Report of Tax Liability for Semiweekly Schedule Depositors,* and attach it to Form 941.

Part 3: Tell us about your business. If a question does NOT apply to your business, leave it blank.

18 If your business has closed or you stopped paying wages . . . . ☐ Check here, and

enter the final date you paid wages [/   /   ] .

19 If you are a seasonal employer and you do not have to file a return for every quarter of the year . ☐ Check here.

Part 4: May we speak with your third-party designee?

Do you want to allow an employee, a paid tax preparer, or another person to discuss this return with the IRS? See the instructions for details.

☐ Yes. Designee's name and phone number [   ] (___) ___ – _____

Select a 5-digit Personal Identification Number (PIN) to use when talking to the IRS. ☐☐☐☐☐

☐ No.

Part 5: Sign here. You MUST complete both pages of Form 941 and SIGN it.

Under penalties of perjury, I declare that I have examined this return, including accompanying schedules and statements, and to the best of my knowledge and belief, it is true, correct, and complete. Declaration of preparer (other than taxpayer) is based on all information of which preparer has any knowledge.

X **Sign your name here** [   ]

Print your name here [   ]

Print your title here [   ]

Date [/   /   ]

Best daytime phone (___) ___ – _____

Paid preparer's use only

Check if you are self-employed . . . . . ☐

Preparer's name	[ ]	Preparer's SSN/PTIN	[ ]
Preparer's signature	[ ]	Date	[/ /]
Firm's name (or yours if self-employed)	[ ]	EIN	[ ]
Address	[ ]	Phone	(___) ___ – _____
City	[ ] State [ ]	ZIP code	[ ]

9

SALES AND CASH RECEIPTS

INSTANT REPLAY: SELF-REVIEW QUIZ 9-1

1. _____ 2. _____ 3. _____ 4. _____ 5. _____

INSTANT REPLAY:
SELF-REVIEW QUIZ 9-2

BERNIE COMPANY
GENERAL JOURNAL

PAGE 1

Date	Account Titles and Description	PR	Dr.	Cr.

ACCOUNTS RECEIVABLE SUBSIDIARY LEDGER

NAME   LEE CORP.

ADDRESS   118 MORRIS RD., BOSTON, MA 01935

Date	Explanation	Post Ref.	Debit	Credit	Dr. Balance

NAME   RING COMPANY

ADDRESS   31 NORRIS ROAD, BOSTON, MA 01935

Date	Explanation	Post Ref.	Debit	Credit	Dr. Balance

PARTIAL GENERAL LEDGER

ACCOUNT RECEIVABLE   ACCOUNT NO. 141

Date		Explanation	Post Ref.	Debit	Credit	Balance	
						Debit	Credit

SALES   ACCOUNT NO. 310

Date		Explanation	Post Ref.	Debit	Credit	Balance	
						Debit	Credit

SALES RETURNS AND ALLOWANCES   ACCOUNT NO. 312

Date		Explanation	Post Ref.	Debit	Credit	Balance	
						Debit	Credit

INSTANT REPLAY: SELF-REVIEW QUIZ 9-3

MABEL CORPORATION
GENERAL JOURNAL

PAGE 3

Date	Account Titles and Description	PR	Dr.	Cr.

PARTIAL GENERAL LEDGER

CASH   ACCOUNT NO. 110

Date 201X		Explanation	Post Ref.	Debit	Credit	Balance Debit	Balance Credit
May	1	Balance	✔			6 0 0 00	

ACCOUNTS RECEIVABLE   ACCOUNT NO. 120

Date 201X		Explanation	Post Ref.	Debit	Credit	Balance Debit	Balance Credit
May	1	Balance	✔			7 0 0 00	

STORE EQUIPMENT   ACCOUNT NO. 130

Date 201X		Explanation	Post Ref.	Debit	Credit	Balance Debit	Balance Credit
May	1	Balance	✔			6 0 0 00	

SALES   ACCOUNT NO. 410

Date 201X		Explanation	Post Ref.	Debit	Credit	Balance Debit	Balance Credit
May	1	Balance	✔				7 0 0 00

SALES DISCOUNT   ACCOUNT NO. <u>420</u>

Date 201X	Explanation	Post Ref.	Debit	Credit	Balance Debit	Balance Credit

NAME   JANIS FROSS

ADDRESS   81 FOSTER RD., BEVERLY, MA 09125

Date 201X	Explanation	Post Ref.	Debit	Credit	Dr. Balance
May 1	Balance	✔			2 0 0 00

ACCOUNTS RECEIVABLE SUBSIDIARY LEDGER

NAME   IRENE WELCH

ADDRESS   10 RONG RD., BEVERLY, MA 01215

Date 201X	Explanation	Post Ref.	Debit	Credit	Dr. Balance
May 1	Balance	✔			5 0 0 00

CHAPTER 9
CONCEPT CHECK

1.

2.

3.

A. _____ _____ _____

B. _____ _____ _____

C. _____ _____ _____

4.

5.

Date		Account Titles and Description	PR	Dr.					Cr.				

6.

PINE CO.
SCHEDULE OF ACCOUNTS RECEIVABLE
MAY 31, 201X

FORMS FOR EXERCISES A OR B

9A-1 OR 9B-1.

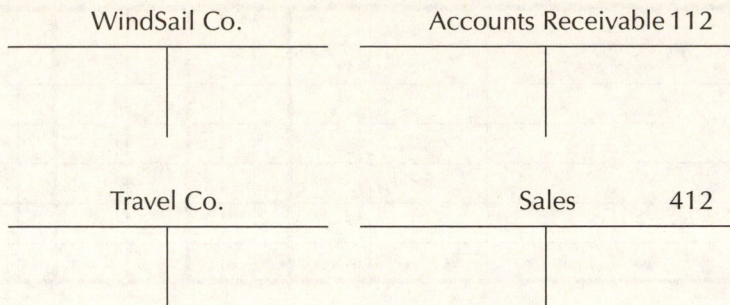

| WindSail Co. | Accounts Receivable 112 |

| Travel Co. | Sales   412 |

9A-2 OR 9B-2.

GENERAL JOURNAL

PAGE 1

Date	Account Titles and Description	PR	Dr.	Cr.

| Glenda Co. | Sales   411 |

| Pearl Co. | Accounts Receivable 112 | Sales Returns & Allowances 412 |

EXERCISES (CONTINUED)

9A-3 OR 9B-3.

9A-4 OR 9B-4.

ANDREW CO.
GENERAL JOURNAL

PAGE 1

Date		Account Titles and Description	PR	Dr.			Cr.		

EXERCISES (CONCLUDED)

	GENERAL JOURNAL (CONTINUED)				PAGE 1
Date	Account Titles and Description	PR	Dr.	Cr.	

ACCOUNTS RECEIVABLE SUBSIDIARY LEDGER

Greenfield Co.

Robert Co.

PARTIAL GENERAL LEDGER

Cash   111

Accounts Receivable   113

Andrew Albright, Capital 311

Sales   411

Sales Returns &
Allowances   412

Sales Discount   413

ANDREW CO.
SCHEDULE OF ACCOUNTS RECEIVABLE
October 31, 201X

_____

_____

_____

9A-5 OR 9B-5.

_____

_____

_____

END OF CHAPTER PROBLEMS

PROBLEM 9A-1 OR PROBLEM 9B-1

CIABATTA AND WHATNOT
GENERAL JOURNAL

PAGE 1

Date	Account Titles and Description	PR	Dr.	Cr.

PROBLEM 9A-1 OR PROBLEM 9B-1 (CONTINUED)

ACCOUNTS RECEIVABLE SUBSIDIARY LEDGER

NAME   CANADIAN CO.

ADDRESS   942 MOSE ST., REVERE, MA 01938

Date	Explanation	Post Ref.	Debit	Credit	Dr. Balance

NAME   CINDI CO.

ADDRESS   8 JOSS AVE., LYNN, MA 01947

Date	Explanation	Post Ref.	Debit	Credit	Dr. Balance

NAME   COMMON LAW CO.

ADDRESS   10 LOST RD., TOPSFIELD, MA 01998

Date	Explanation	Post Ref.	Debit	Credit	Dr. Balance

PROBLEM 9A-1 OR PROBLEM 9B-1 (CONTINUED)

CIABATTA AND WHATNOT
GENERAL LEDGER

ACCOUNTS RECEIVABLE   **ACCOUNT NO. 112**

Date	Explanation	Post Ref.	Debit	Credit	Balance Debit	Balance Credit

BREAD SALES   **ACCOUNT NO. 410**

Date	Explanation	Post Ref.	Debit	Credit	Balance Debit	Balance Credit

GROCERY SALES   **ACCOUNT NO. 411**

Date	Explanation	Post Ref.	Debit	Credit	Balance Debit	Balance Credit

SALES RETURNS AND ALLOWANCES   **ACCOUNT NO. 412**

Date	Explanation	Post Ref.	Debit	Credit	Balance Debit	Balance Credit

PROBLEM 9A-1 OR PROBLEM 9B-1 (CONCLUDED)

CIABATTA AND WHATNOT
SCHEDULE OF ACCOUNTS RECEIVABLE
JANUARY 31, 201X

PROBLEM 9A-2 OR PROBLEM 9B-2

JACK'S AUTO SUPPLY
GENERAL JOURNAL

PAGE 2

Date	Account Titles and Description	PR	Dr.	Cr.

PROBLEM 9A-2 OR PROBLEM 9B-2 (CONTINUED)

ACCOUNTS RECEIVABLE SUBSIDIARY LEDGER

NAME   R. DANIELSON

ADDRESS   9 ROE ST., BARTLETT, NH 01382

Date	Explanation	Post Ref.	Debit	Credit	Dr. Balance
	Balance				

NAME   J. WALLACE

ADDRESS   22 REESE ST., LACONIA, NH 04321

Date	Explanation	Post Ref.	Debit	Credit	Dr. Balance

NAME   L. WHITNALL

ADDRESS   12 ASTER RD., MERRIMACK, NH 02134

Date	Explanation	Post Ref.	Debit	Credit	Dr. Balance

PROBLEM 9A-2 OR PROBLEM 9B-2 (CONTINUED)

JACK'S AUTO SUPPLY
PARTIAL GENERAL LEDGER

ACCOUNTS RECEIVABLE   ACCOUNT NO. 110

Date	Explanation	Post Ref.	Debit	Credit	Balance Debit	Balance Credit

SALES TAX PAYABLE   ACCOUNT NO. 210

Date	Explanation	Post Ref.	Debit	Credit	Balance Debit	Balance Credit

AUTO PARTS SALES   ACCOUNT NO. 410

Date	Explanation	Post Ref.	Debit	Credit	Balance Debit	Balance Credit

SALES RETURNS AND ALLOWANCES   ACCOUNT NO. 420

Date	Explanation	Post Ref.	Debit	Credit	Balance Debit	Balance Credit

PROBLEM 9A-2 OR PROBLEM 9B-2 (CONCLUDED)

(3)

JACK'S AUTO SUPPLY
SCHEDULE OF ACCOUNTS RECEIVABLE
NOVEMBER 30, 201X

PROBLEM 9A-3 OR PROBLEM 9B-3
(1,2)

PATTERN'S SNEAKER SHOP
GENERAL JOURNAL

PAGE 2

Date		Account Titles and Description	PR	Dr.		Cr.	

PROBLEM 9A-3 OR PROBLEM 9B-3 (CONTINUED)
(1,2)

PATTERN'S SNEAKER SHOP
GENERAL JOURNAL

PAGE 3

Date	Account Titles and Description	PR	Dr.	Cr.

PROBLEM 9A-3 OR PROBLEM 9B-3 (CONTINUED)

ACCOUNTS RECEIVABLE SUBSIDIARY LEDGER

NAME   B.DONATI

ADDRESS   1822 RIVER RD., MEMPHIS, TN 09111

Date	Explanation	Post Ref.	Debit	Credit	Dr. Balance

NAME   RON LINDALL

ADDRESS   18 MASS. AVE., SAN DIEGO, CA 01999

Date	Explanation	Post Ref.	Debit	Credit	Dr. Balance

ACCOUNTS RECEIVABLE SUBSIDIARY LEDGER

NAME   PAM PILAR

ADDRESS   918 MOORE DR., HOMEWOOD, IL 60430

Date	Explanation	Post Ref.	Debit	Credit	Dr. Balance

PROBLEM 9A-3 OR PROBLEM 9B-3 (CONTINUED)

NAME JIM ZAMORA

ADDRESS 2 CHESTNUT ST., SWAMPSCOTT, MA 01970

Date		Explanation	Post Ref.	Debit	Credit	Dr. Balance

PATTERN'S SNEAKER SHOP
PARTIAL GENERAL LEDGER

CASH   ACCOUNT NO. 10

Date		Explanation	Post Ref.	Debit	Credit	Balance	
						Debit	Credit

PROBLEM 9A-3 OR PROBLEM 9B-3 (CONTINUED)

ACCOUNTS RECEIVABLE   **ACCOUNT NO. 12**

Date	Explanation	Post Ref.	Debit	Credit	Balance Debit	Balance Credit

SNEAKER RACK EQUIPMENT   **ACCOUNT NO. 14**

Date	Explanation	Post Ref.	Debit	Credit	Balance Debit	Balance Credit

MIKE PATTERN, CAPITAL   **ACCOUNT NO.**

Date	Explanation	Post Ref.	Debit	Credit	Balance Debit	Balance Credit

PROBLEM 9A-3 OR PROBLEM 9B-3 (CONTINUED)

SALES   ACCOUNT NO. 40

Date	Explanation	Post Ref.	Debit	Credit	Balance	
					Debit	Credit

SALES DISCOUNT   ACCOUNT NO. 42

Date 201X	Explanation	Post Ref.	Debit	Credit	Balance	
					Debit	Credit

SALES RETURNS & ALLOWANCES   ACCOUNT NO. 44

Date 201X	Explanation	Post Ref.	Debit	Credit	Balance	
					Debit	Credit

PROBLEM 9A-3 OR PROBLEM 9B-3 (CONCLUDED)

(3)

PATTERN'S SNEAKER SHOP
SCHEDULE OF ACCOUNTS RECEIVABLE
MAY 31, 201X

Name _____ Class _____ Date _____

PROBLEM 9A-4 OR PROBLEM 9B-4

GARY'S COSMETIC MARKET
GENERAL JOURNAL

PAGE 1

Date	Account Titles and Description	PR	Dr.	Cr.

PROBLEM 9A-4 OR PROBLEM 9B-4 (CONTINUED)

GARY'S COSMETIC MARKET
GENERAL JOURNAL

Date	Account Titles and Description	PR	Dr.	Cr.

PROBLEM 9A-4 OR PROBLEM 9B-4 (CONTINUED)

ACCOUNTS RECEIVABLE SUBSIDIARY LEDGER

NAME   PETER MELNYK CO.

ADDRESS   2 RYAN RD., BUFFALO, NY 09113

Date		Explanation	Post Ref.	Debit	Credit	Debit Balance

PROBLEM 9A-4 OR PROBLEM 9B-4 (CONTINUED)

ACCOUNTS RECEIVABLE SUBSIDIARY LEDGER

NAME   MARIKA SANFORD CO.

ADDRESS   4 REEL RD., LANCASTER, PA 04332

Date		Explanation	Post Ref.	Debit	Credit	Debit Balance

NAME   MARY RUVOLO CO.

ADDRESS   14 BONE DR., ENGLEWOOD CLIFFS, NJ 07632

Date		Explanation	Post Ref.	Debit	Credit	Debit Balance

NAME   FIONE TAY CO.

ADDRESS   2 MARION RD., BOSTON, MA 01981

Date		Explanation	Post Ref.	Debit	Credit	Debit Balance

PROBLEM 9A-4 OR PROBLEM 9B-4 (CONTINUED)

GARY'S COSMETIC MARKET
GENERAL LEDGER

CASH   ACCOUNT NO. 10

Date	Explanation	Post Ref.	Debit	Credit	Balance Debit	Balance Credit

ACCOUNTS RECEIVABLE   ACCOUNT NO. 12

Date	Explanation	Post Ref.	Debit	Credit	Balance Debit	Balance Credit

PROBLEM 9A-4 OR PROBLEM 9B-4 (CONTINUED)

SALES TAX PAYABLE   ACCOUNT NO. 20

Date	Explanation	Post Ref.	Debit	Credit	Balance Debit	Balance Credit

GARY WILCOX, CAPITAL   ACCOUNT NO. 30

Date	Explanation	Post Ref.	Debit	Credit	Balance Debit	Balance Credit

LIPSTICK SALES   ACCOUNT NO. 40

Date	Explanation	Post Ref.	Debit	Credit	Balance Debit	Balance Credit

PROBLEM 9A-4 OR PROBLEM 9B-4 (CONCLUDED)

SALES RETURNS & ALLOWANCES, LIPSTICK   ACCOUNT NO. 42

Date		Explanation	Post Ref.	Debit	Credit	Balance Debit	Balance Credit

EYE SHADOW SALES   ACCOUNT NO. 44

Date		Explanation	Post Ref.	Debit	Credit	Balance Debit	Balance Credit

(3)

GARY'S COSMETIC MARKET
SCHEDULE OF ACCOUNTS RECEIVABLE
OCTOBER 31, 201X

CHAPTER 9
SUMMARY PRACTICE TEST
SALES AND CASH RECEIPTS

Part I Instructions

Fill in the blank(s) to complete the statement.

1. The normal balance of sales returns and allowances is _____.
2. _____ _____ and _____ is a contra-revenue account.
3. Sales is a(n) _____ account.
4. A discount period is less time than the _____ _____.
5. A debit to accounts receivable and a credit to sales records the sale of merchandise _____ _____.
6. The _____ _____ _____ _____ lists in alphabetical order an account for each customer.
7. _____ _____ in the general ledger is called the controlling account.
8. The (✔) in the PR column of the general journal indicates that the accounts receivable ledger has been updated _____ _____ _____.
9. Issuing _____ _____ results in a debit to sales returns and allowancs and a credit to accounts receivable.
10. In a wholesale company there is no _____ tax.
11. Sales Tax Payable is a(n) _____ in the general ledger.
12. Cash sales result in a(n) _____ to cash and a _____ to sales.
13. Sales Returns and Allowances is a(n) _____ _____ account.
14. The _____ _____ has to be posted to the general as well as the sales ledger.
15. No _____ _____ are taken on sales tax.
16. A(n) _____ _____ _____ _____ lists the ending balances from the accounts receivable ledger.

Part II

Complete the following chart:

Transaction	Dr.	Cr.
1. Sale for cash	_____	_____
2. Issued credit memo	_____	_____
3. Sale on account	_____	_____
4. Received cash payment less discount	_____	_____

Partial Chart of Accounts

10 Cash	40 Sales
20 Accounts Receivable	42 Sales Discount
	44 Sales Returns and Allowances

Part III Instructions

Answer true or false to the following statements.

1. A schedule of accounts receivable shows what customers do not owe.
2. A perpetual system would keep continual track of inventory.
3. Sales Discount policies can never change.
4. Sales Tax Payable is an asset.
5. Sales Discount is a contra asset.
6. Issuing a credit memorandum results in Sales, Returns and Allowances decreasing with Accounts Receivable increasing.
7. The sum of the accounts receivable subsidiary ledger is equal to the balance in the controlling account at the end of the month.
8. The buyer issues the credit memo.
9. The accounts receivable subsidiary ledger is listed in numerical order.
10. Sales Discount is a contra-revenue account.
11. Net sales = gross sales – SRA-SD.
12. The normal balance of an Accounts Receivable ledger is a debit.
13. Discounts are taken on sales tax.
14. 2/10, N/30 means a cash discount is good for 30 days.
15. The accounts receivable subsidiary ledger is always located in the general ledger.
16. Gross profit plus operating expenses equals net income.
17. A credit period is longer than the discount period.
18. In the accounts receivable subsidiary ledger each account is debited to record amounts customers owe.
19. Sales Tax Payable is an asset.

CHAPTER 9
SOLUTIONS TO SUMMARY PRACTICE TEST

Part I

1. debit
2. Sales Returns, Allowances
3. revenue
4. credit period
5. on account
6. accounts receivable subsidiary ledger
7. Accounts Receivable
8. during the month
9. credit memorandum
10. sales
11. liability
12. debit, credit
13. contra-revenue
14. journalized transaction
15. cash discounts
16. schedule of accounts receivable

Part II

	Dr.	Cr.
1.	10	40
2.	44	20
3.	20	40
4.	10	20
	42	

Part III

1.	false	**11.**	true
2.	true	**12.**	true
3.	false	**13.**	false
4.	false	**14.**	false
5.	false	**15.**	false
6.	false	**16.**	false
7.	true	**17.**	true
8.	false	**18.**	true
9.	false	**19.**	false
10.	true		

CONTINUING PROBLEM—ON THE JOB FOR CHAPTER 9

SANCHEZ COMPUTER CENTER
GENERAL JOURNAL

PAGE 7

Date	Account Titles and Description	PR	Dr.	Cr.

SANCHEZ COMPUTER CENTER
SCHEDULE OF ACCOUNTS RECEIVABLE
1/31/1X

CASH   ACCOUNT NO. **1000**

Date		Explanation	Post Ref.	Debit	Credit	Balance Debit	Balance Credit
1/1	1X	Balance Forward	✔			3 3 3 6 64	

SANCHEZ COMPUTER CENTER
PARTIAL GENERAL LEDGER

ACCOUNTS RECEIVABLE   **ACCOUNT NO. 1020**

Date		Explanation	Post Ref.	Debit	Credit	Balance Debit	Balance Credit
1/1	1X	Balance Forward	✔			13 600 00	

SALES   **ACCOUNT NO. 4010**

Date		Explanation	Post Ref.	Debit	Credit	Balance Debit	Balance Credit

SALES RETURNS & ALLOWANCES   **ACCOUNT NO. 4020**

Date		Explanation	Post Ref.	Debit	Credit	Balance Debit	Balance Credit

SALES DISCOUNTS ACCOUNT NO. <u>4030</u>

Date		Explanation	Post Ref.	Debit	Credit	Balance	
						Debit	Credit

ACCOUNTS RECEIVABLE
SUBSIDIARY LEDGER

NAME   TAYLOR GOLF   **ACCOUNT NO. 100**

ADDRESS   1010 MOCKINGBIRD LANE, CARLSBAD, CA 92008

Date		Explanation	Post Ref.	Debit	Credit	Dr. Balance
1/1	1X	Balance forward	✔			2 9 0 0 00

NAME   VITA NEEDLE   **ACCOUNT NO. 101**

ADDRESS   144 CANTATA, IRVINE, CA 92606

Date		Explanation	Post Ref.	Debit	Credit	Dr. Balance
1/1	1X	Balance	✔			6 8 0 0 00

ACCOUNTS RECEIVABLE SUBSIDIARY LEDGER

NAME   ACCU PAC   **ACCOUNT NO. 103**

ADDRESS   1717 JORDAN ST., SAN CLEMENTE, CA 91607

Date		Explanation	Post Ref.	Debit	Credit	Dr. Balance
1/1	1X	Balance	✔			3 9 0 0 00

NAME   ANTHONY J. PITALE   **ACCOUNT NO. 104**

ADDRESS   600 NEWPORT BEACH, NEWPORT, CA 91600

Date		Explanation	Post Ref.	Debit	Credit	Dr. Balance

10

PURCHASES AND CASH PAYMENTS

INSTANT REPLAY: SELF-REVIEW QUIZ 10-1

1. _____ 2. _____ 3. _____ 4. _____ 5. _____

INSTANT REPLAY: SELF-REVIEW QUIZ 10-2

MUNROE CO.
GENERAL JOURNAL

PAGE 1

Date	Account Titles and Description	PR	Dr.	Cr.

ACCOUNTS PAYABLE SUBSIDIARY LEDGER

NAME **JOHN BUTLER COMPANY**

ADDRESS **18 REED RD., HOMEWOOD, IL 60430**

Date	Explanation	Post Ref.	Debit	Credit	Cr. Balance

NAME **FLYNN COMPANY**

ADDRESS **15 FOSS AVE., ENGLEWOOD CLIFFS, NJ 07632**

Date	Explanation	Post Ref.	Debit	Credit	Cr. Balance

PARTIAL GENERAL LEDGER

EQUIPMENT **ACCOUNT NO. 121**

Date	Explanation	Post Ref.	Debit	Credit	Balance	
					Debit	Credit

ACCOUNTS PAYABLE   ACCOUNT NO. 212

Date		Explanation	Post Ref.	Debit	Credit	Balance	
						Debit	Credit

PURCHASES   ACCOUNT NO. 512

Date		Explanation	Post Ref.	Debit	Credit	Balance	
						Debit	Credit

PURCHASES RETURNS AND ALLOWANCES   ACCOUNT NO. 513

Date		Explanation	Post Ref.	Debit	Credit	Balance	
						Debit	Credit

INSTANT REPLAY: SELF-REVIEW QUIZ 10-3

MELISSA COMPANY
GENERAL JOURNAL

PAGE 2

Date	Account Titles and Description	PR	Dr.	Cr.

ACCOUNTS PAYABLE SUBSIDARY LEDGER

NAME   **BOB FINKELSTEIN**

ADDRESS   **112 FLYING HIGHWAY, TRENTON, NJ 00861**

Date 201X		Explanation	Post Ref.	Debit	Credit	Cr. Balance
June	1	Balance	✔			3 0 0 00

NAME   **AL JEEP**

ADDRESS   **118 WANG RD., SAUGUS, MA 01432**

Date 201X		Explanation	Post Ref.	Debit	Credit	Cr. Balance
June	1	Balance	✔			2 0 0 00

PARTIAL GENERAL LEDGER

CASH **ACCOUNT NO. 110**

Date 201X		Explanation	Post Ref.	Debit	Credit	Balance Debit	Balance Credit
June	1	Balance	✔			7 0 0 00	

ACCOUNTS PAYABLE **ACCOUNT NO. 210**

Date 201X		Explanation	Post Ref.	Debit	Credit	Balance Debit	Balance Credit
June	1	Balance	✔				5 0 0 00

PURCHASES DISCOUNT **ACCOUNT NO. 511**

Date	Explanation	Post Ref.	Debit	Credit	Balance Debit	Balance Credit

ADVERTISING EXPENSE **ACCOUNT NO. 610**

Date	Explanation	Post Ref.	Debit	Credit	Balance Debit	Balance Credit

INSTANT REPLAY: SELF-REVIEW QUIZ 10-4

PETE'S CLOCK SHOP
GENERAL JOURNAL

Date	Account Titles and Description	PR	Dr.	Cr.

PETE'S CLOCK SHOP
GENERAL JOURNAL

PAGE 3

Date		Account Titles and Description	PR	Dr.				Cr.			

CHAPTER 10
CONCEPT CHECK

1. A. _____   D. _____

    B. _____   E. _____

    C. _____   F. _____

2.

3. _____

    _____

    _____

    _____

    _____

    _____

    _____

    _____

4. A. _____

    B. _____

    C. _____

5.

6.

MATTHEW.COM
SCHEDULE OF ACCOUNTS PAYABLE
MAY 31, 201X

7.

_____

_____

8, 9, 10

Date		Account Titles and Description	PR	Dr.			Cr.		

FORMS FOR EXERCISES A OR B

10A-1 OR 10B-1.

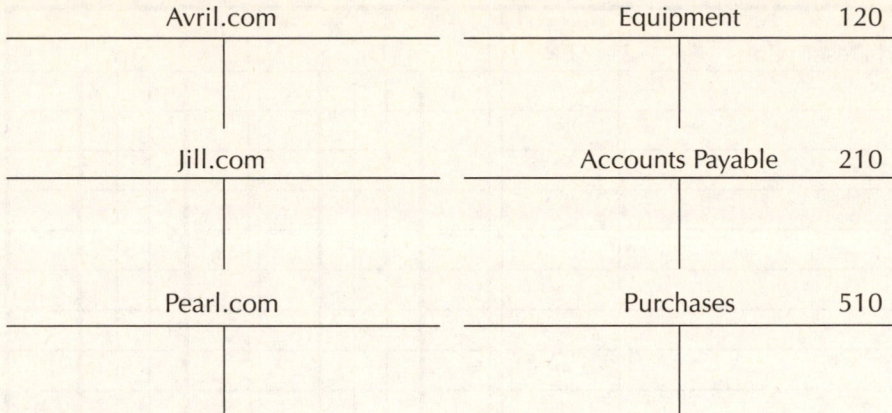

Avril.com		Equipment 120
Jill.com		Accounts Payable 210
Pearl.com		Purchases 510

10A-2 OR 10B-2.   PAGE 1

| Mango Co. | Accounts Payable 211 | Purchases Returns and Allowances 513 |

EXERCISES (CONTINUED)

10A-3 OR 10B-3.

Date		Account Titles and Description	PR		Dr.					Cr.			

ACCOUNTS PAYABLE SUBSIDIARY LEDGER

A. Jenkins
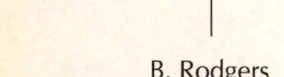

B. Foss

J. Lee

B. Rodgers

PARTIAL GENERAL LEDGER

Cash   110

Accounts Payable   210

Purchases Discount   511

Advertising Expense   610

EXERCISES (CONTINUED)

10A-4 OR 10B-4.

KADEN'S CLOTHING
SCHEDULE OF ACCOUNTS PAYABLE
APRIL 30, 201X

_____
_____
_____
_____

Accounts Payable   210

10A-5 OR 10B-5.

Accounts Affected	Category	↑↓	Rules

10A-6 OR 10B-6.

_____
_____
_____
_____
_____

FORM FOR EXERCISES 10A-7 OR 10B-7, 10A-8 OR 10B-8, 10A-9 OR 10B-9, 10A-10 OR 10B-10

Date	Account Titles and Description	PR	Dr.	Cr.

FORM FOR EXERCISES 10A-7 OR 10B-7, 10A-8 OR 10B-8, 10A-9 OR 10B-9, 10A-10 OR 10B-10 (CONTINUED)

Date		Account Titles and Description	PR		Dr.			Cr.		

CALCULATIONS PAGE

END OF CHAPTER PROBLEMS

PROBLEM 10A-1 OR PROBLEM 10B-1

RODNEY'S SKATE SHOP
GENERAL JOURNAL

PAGE 2

Date	Account Titles and Description	PR	Dr.	Cr.

PROBLEM 10A-1 OR PROBLEM 10B-1 (CONTINUED)

ACCOUNTS PAYABLE SUBSIDIARY LEDGER

NAME   ADAMS.COM

ADDRESS   12 SMITH ST., DEARBORN, MI 09113

Date	Explanation	Post Ref.	Debit	Credit	Cr. Balance

NAME   NORTON CO.

ADDRESS   1 RANTOUL RD., CHARLOTTE, NC 01114

Date	Explanation	Post Ref.	Debit	Credit	Cr. Balance

NAME   ROLO CO.

ADDRESS   2 WEST RD., LYNN, MA 01471

Date	Explanation	Post Ref.	Debit	Credit	Cr. Balance

PARTIAL GENERAL LEDGER

STORE SUPPLIES   ACCOUNT NO. 115

Date	Explanation	Post Ref.	Debit	Credit	Balance Debit	Balance Credit

PROBLEM 10A-1 OR PROBLEM 10B-1 (CONCLUDED)

STORE EQUIPMENT   **ACCOUNT NO. 121**

Date		Explanation	Post Ref.	Debit	Credit	Balance	
						Debit	Credit

ACCOUNTS PAYABLE   **ACCOUNT NO. 210**

Date		Explanation	Post Ref.	Debit	Credit	Balance	
						Debit	Credit

PURCHASES   **ACCOUNT NO. 510**

Date		Explanation	Post Ref.	Debit	Credit	Balance	
						Debit	Credit

Name _____ Class _____ Date _____

PROBLEM 10A-2 OR PROBLEM 10B-2

RACHEL'S NATURAL FOOD

Date	Account Titles and Description	PR	Dr.	Cr.

PROBLEM 10A-2 OR PROBLEM 10B-2 (CONTINUED)

ACCOUNTS PAYABLE SUBSIDIARY LEDGER

NAME   AIRON CO.

ADDRESS   11 LYNNWAY AVE., NEWPORT, RI 03112

Date		Explanation	Post Ref.	Debit	Credit	Cr. Balance

NAME   BIXBY CO.

ADDRESS   21 RIVER ST., ANAHEIM, CA 43110

Date		Explanation	Post Ref.	Debit	Credit	Cr. Balance

NAME   MIXON CO.

ADDRESS   10 ASTER RD., DUBUQUE, IA 80021

Date		Explanation	Post Ref.	Debit	Credit	Cr. Balance

NAME   RYAN CO.

ADDRESS   22 GERALD RD., SMITH, CO 43138

Date		Explanation	Post Ref.	Debit	Credit	Cr. Balance

PROBLEM 10A-2 OR PROBLEM 10B-2 (CONTINUED)

PARTIAL GENERAL LEDGER

STORE SUPPLIES   ACCOUNT NO. 110

Date	Explanation	Post Ref.	Debit	Credit	Balance Debit	Balance Credit

OFFICE EQUIPMENT   ACCOUNT NO. 120

Date	Explanation	Post Ref.	Debit	Credit	Balance Debit	Balance Credit

ACCOUNTS PAYABLE   ACCOUNT NO. 210

Date	Explanation	Post Ref.	Debit	Credit	Balance Debit	Balance Credit

PURCHASES   ACCOUNT NO. 510

Date	Explanation	Post Ref.	Debit	Credit	Balance Debit	Balance Credit

PROBLEM 10A-2 OR PROBLEM 10B-2 (CONCLUDED)

PURCHASES RETURNS AND ALLOWANCES   ACCOUNT NO. 512

Date		Explanation	Post Ref.	Debit	Credit	Balance	
						Debit	Credit

RACHEL'S NATURAL FOOD

SCHEDULE OF ACCOUNTS PAYABLE
AUGUST 31, 201X

PROBLEM 10A-3 OR PROBLEM 10B-3

Date		Account Titles and Description	PR	Dr.		Cr.	

PROBLEM 10A-3 OR PROBLEM 10B-3 (CONTINUED)

ACCOUNTS PAYABLE SUBSIDIARY LEDGER

NAME   ANDREWS CO.

ADDRESS   1 REACH RD., IPSWICH, MA 01932

Date	Explanation	Post Ref.	Debit	Credit	Cr. Balance

NAME   HITCH CO.

ADDRESS   1 RALPH RD., REVERE, MA 01321

Date	Explanation	Post Ref.	Debit	Credit	Cr. Balance

NAME   SEAKATE CO.

ADDRESS   7 PLYMOUTH AVE., GLENN, NH 01218

Date	Explanation	Post Ref.	Debit	Credit	Cr. Balance

NAME   ZEKE CO.

ADDRESS   22 REY RD., BOCA RATON, FL 99132

Date	Explanation	Post Ref.	Debit	Credit	Cr. Balance

PROBLEM 10A-3 OR PROBLEM 10B-3 (CONTINUED)

PARTIAL GENERAL LEDGER

CASH   ACCOUNT NO. 110

Date	Explanation	Post Ref.	Debit	Credit	Balance Debit	Balance Credit

DELIVERY TRUCK   ACCOUNT NO. 150

Date 201X	Explanation	Post Ref.	Debit	Credit	Balance Debit	Balance Credit

ACCOUNTS PAYABLE   ACCOUNT NO. 210

Date	Explanation	Post Ref.	Debit	Credit	Balance Debit	Balance Credit

COMPUTER PURCHASES   ACCOUNT NO. 510

Date 201X	Explanation	Post Ref.	Debit	Credit	Balance Debit	Balance Credit

PROBLEM 10A-3 OR PROBLEM 10B-3 (CONCLUDED)

COMPUTER PURCHASES DISCOUNT   **ACCOUNT NO. 511**

Date		Explanation	Post Ref.	Debit	Credit	Balance	
						Debit	Credit

RENT EXPENSE   **ACCOUNT NO. 610**

Date		Explanation	Post Ref.	Debit	Credit	Balance	
						Debit	Credit

UTILITIES EXPENSE   **ACCOUNT NO. 620**

Date		Explanation	Post Ref.	Debit	Credit	Balance	
						Debit	Credit

ELLIS COMPUTER CENTER
SCHEDULE OF ACCOUNTS PAYABLE
OCTOBER 31, 201X

PROBLEM 10A-4 OR PROBLEM 10B-4

(1)

ALLISON'S TOY HOUSE
GENERAL JOURNAL

PAGE 1

Date	Account Titles and Description	PR	Dr.	Cr.

PROBLEM 10A-4 OR PROBLEM 10B-4 (CONTINUED)

Date		Account Titles and Description	PR		Dr.			Cr.	

PROBLEM 10A-4 OR PROBLEM 10B-4 (CONTINUED)

Date		Account Titles and Description	PR		Dr.			Cr.	

PROBLEM 10A-4 OR PROBLEM 10B-4 (CONTINUED)

Date		Account Titles and Description	PR		Dr.				Cr.			

PROBLEM 10A-4 OR PROBLEM 10B-4 (CONTINUED)

Date		Account Titles and Description	PR	Dr.	Cr.

PROBLEM 10A-4 OR PROBLEM 10B-4 (CONTINUED)

(2)   ACCOUNTS PAYABLE SUBSIDIARY LEDGER

NAME   LANE CHIPKIN

ADDRESS   87 GARFIELD AVE., REVERE, MA 01245

Date	Explanation	Post Ref.	Debit	Credit	Cr. Balance

NAME   SAM KATZ GARAGE

ADDRESS   22 REGIS RD., BOSTON, MA 01950

Date	Explanation	Post Ref.	Debit	Credit	Cr. Balance

NAME   SARAH HARMITZ CO.

ADDRESS   22 RETTER ST., SAN DIEGO, CA 01211

Date	Explanation	Post Ref.	Debit	Credit	Cr. Balance

NAME   WILLIAM SMITH

ADDRESS   2 SPRING ST., WEERS, ND 02118

Date	Explanation	Post Ref.	Debit	Credit	Cr. Balance

PROBLEM 10A-4 OR PROBLEM 10B-4 (CONTINUED)

ACCOUNTS RECEIVABLE SUBSIDIARY LEDGER

NAME   ROBERT GIBBS

ADDRESS   24 RYAN RD., BUIKE, OH 02183

Date	Explanation	Post Ref.	Debit	Credit	Dr. Balance

NAME   BONNIE FLOW CO.

ADDRESS   2 SMITH RD., DALLAS, TX 22210

Date	Explanation	Post Ref.	Debit	Credit	Dr. Balance

NAME   INEZ TENENBAUM

ADDRESS   1 SCHOOL ST., CLEVELAND, OH 22441

Date	Explanation	Post Ref.	Debit	Credit	Dr. Balance

PROBLEM 10A-4 OR PROBLEM 10B-4 (CONTINUED)

NAME   AMANDA READER

ADDRESS   18 VEEK RD., CHESTER, CT 80111

Date	Explanation	Post Ref.	Debit	Credit	Dr. Balance

GENERAL LEDGER

CASH   ACCOUNT NO. 110

Date	Explanation	Post Ref.	Debit	Credit	Balance Debit	Balance Credit

PROBLEM 10A-4 OR PROBLEM 10B-4 (CONTINUED)

ACCOUNTS RECEIVABLE   ACCOUNT NO. 112

Date	Explanation	Post Ref.	Debit	Credit	Balance Debit	Balance Credit

PREPAID RENT   ACCOUNT NO. 114

Date	Explanation	Post Ref.	Debit	Credit	Balance Debit	Balance Credit

DELIVERY TRUCK   ACCOUNT NO. 121

Date	Explanation	Post Ref.	Debit	Credit	Balance Debit	Balance Credit

PROBLEM 10A-4 OR PROBLEM 10B-4 (CONTINUED)

ACCOUNTS PAYABLE   ACCOUNT NO. 210

Date	Explanation	Post Ref.	Debit	Credit	Balance Debit	Balance Credit

A. COOPER, CAPITAL   ACCOUNT NO. 310

Date	Explanation	Post Ref.	Debit	Credit	Balance Debit	Balance Credit

TOY SALES   ACCOUNT NO. 410

Date	Explanation	Post Ref.	Debit	Credit	Balance Debit	Balance Credit

PROBLEM 10A-4 OR PROBLEM 10B-4 (CONTINUED)

SALES RETURNS AND ALLOWANCES   ACCOUNT NO. 412

Date	Explanation	Post Ref.	Debit	Credit	Balance Debit	Balance Credit

SALES DISCOUNTS   ACCOUNT NO. 414

Date	Explanation	Post Ref.	Debit	Credit	Balance Debit	Balance Credit

TOY PURCHASES   ACCOUNT NO. 510

Date	Explanation	Post Ref.	Debit	Credit	Balance Debit	Balance Credit

PURCHASES RETURNS AND ALLOWANCES   ACCOUNT NO. 512

Date	Explanation	Post Ref.	Debit	Credit	Balance Debit	Balance Credit

PROBLEM 10A-4 OR PROBLEM 10B-4 (CONTINUED)

PURCHASES DISCOUNT   ACCOUNT NO. 514

Date		Explanation	Post Ref.	Debit	Credit	Balance	
						Debit	Credit

SALARIES EXPENSE   ACCOUNT NO. 610

Date		Explanation	Post Ref.	Debit	Credit	Balance	
						Debit	Credit

CLEANING EXPENSE   ACCOUNT NO. 612

Date		Explanation	Post Ref.	Debit	Credit	Balance	
						Debit	Credit

PROBLEM 10A-4 OR PROBLEM 10B-4 (CONCLUDED)

(3)

ALLISON'S TOY HOUSE
SCHEDULE OF ACCOUNTS RECEIVABLE
OCTOBER 31, 201X

(3)

ALLISON'S TOY HOUSE
SCHEDULE OF ACCOUNTS PAYABLE
OCTOBER 31, 201X

PROBLEM 10A-5 OR PROBLEM 10B-5

PAGE 3

Date	Account Titles and Description	PR	Dr.	Cr.

PROBLEM 10A-5 OR PROBLEM 10B-5 (CONCLUDED)

PAGE 4

Date		Account Titles and Description	PR	Dr.			Cr.		

CHAPTER 10
SUMMARY PRACTICE TEST
PURCHASES AND CASH PAYMENTS

Part I Instructions

Fill in the blank(s) to complete the statement.

1. The trend in accounting is more to _____ inventory rather than _____ inventory.

2. Purchase discounts are categorized as a(n) _____ _____ account.

3. The Purchases account has a _____ balance.

4. Purchases are defined as merchandise for _____ to customers.

5. The accounts payable subsidiary ledger represents a potential _____ of cash.

6. The controlling account in the general ledger for the accounts payable subsidiary ledger is called _____ _____.

7. The accounts payable subsidiary ledger would be recorded _____.

8. The balance in the Accounts Payable controlling account should be equal to the sum of the accounts payable subsidiary ledger accounts _____ _____ _____ _____.

9. In perpetual inventory, purchases are recorded as _____ _____.

10. The ✔ in the reference column indicates that the _____ _____ _____ _____ has been updated.

11. A(n) _____ _____ that is issued means the buyer owes less money, as merchandise is being returned or an allowance received.

12. A debit memorandum issued or a credit memorandum received results in a(n) _____ to Accounts Payable and a credit to Purchases, Returns and Allowances.

13. List price − net price = _____ _____ amount.

14. The accounts payable subsidiary ledger is listed in _____ _____.

15. Purchases Returns and Allowances is increased by a(n) _____.

16. Cost of goods sold is classified as a(n) _____.

17. In a perpetual inventory system, freight is recorded in the _____ _____ account.

18. Purchases Discounts is increased by _____.

19. A(n) _____ _____ provides the purchasing department the information to then prepare a purchase order.

20. A(n) _____ _____ is made out after a company inspects received shipments.

Part II

Complete the following table:

	Account Title	CAT	↑↓	Financial Statement
1.	Purchases			
2.	Purchase Discount			
3.	Accounts Receivable			
4.	Cost of Goods Sold			
5.	Salary Expenses			
6.	Accounts Payable			
7.	Purchase Returns and Allowances			
8.	Cash			
9.	Supplies			
10.	Sale Discount			

Part III Instructions

Answer true or false to the following statements.

1. F.O.B. shipping point means the seller is responsible to cover shipping costs.
2. The Purchases account is a contra-cost of goods sold account.
3. Purchases discounts are the result of paying for equipment within the discount period.
4. F.O.B. Destination means the seller is responsible to cover shipping costs.
5. Purchases discounts are taken on freight.
6. Merchandise inventory is an asset.
7. Cost of goods sold is a cost.
8. The balance in Accounts Payable, the controlling account, will be equal to the sum of the accounts receivable subsidiary ledger at the end of the month.
9. A purchase order is completed after the purchase requisition.
10. On receiving a purchase order, the seller may issue a sales invoice.
11. The normal balance of Purchases Discount is a debit balance.
12. The seller will often issue a debit memorandum to the buyer.
13. Cost of goods sold is used in a periodic inventory system.
14. Returned equipment by a buyer results in a change in Purchases Returns and Allowances.
15. Trade discounts do not occur because of early payments of one's bills.
16. A seller's sales discount on purchases is the buyer's purchases discount.
17. Buying of equipment on account is only recorded in the general ledger.
18. On receiving a debit memorandum, the seller will issue a credit memorandum.
19. Returns in a perpetual accounting system are recorded in the merchandise inventory account.
20. Purchases are contra costs.

CHAPTER 10
SOLUTIONS TO SUMMARY PRACTICE TEST

Part I

1. perpetual, periodic
2. contra-cost
3. debit
4. resale
5. outflow
6. accounts payable
7. daily
8. at end of month
9. merchandise inventory
10. accounts payable subsidiary ledger
11. debit memorandum
12. debit
13. trade discount
14. alphabetical order
15. credit
16. cost
17. merchandise inventory
18. credits
19. purchase requisition
20. receiving report

Part II

1.	cost	Dr	Cr	Income Statement
2.	contra-cost	Cr	Dr	Income Statement
3.	asset	Dr	Cr	Balance Sheet
4.	cost	Dr	Cr	Income Statement
5.	expense	Dr	Cr	Income Statement
6.	liability	Cr	Dr	Balance Sheet
7.	contra-cost	Cr	Dr	Income Statement
8.	asset	Dr	Cr	Balance Sheet
9.	asset	Dr	Cr	Balance Sheet
10.	contra-revenue	Dr	Cr	Income Statement

Part III

1.	false		**11.**	false
2.	false		**12.**	false
3.	true		**13.**	false
4.	true		**14.**	true
5.	false		**15.**	true
6.	true		**16.**	true
7.	true		**17.**	false
8.	false		**18.**	true
9.	true		**19.**	true
10.	true		**20.**	false

CONTINUING PROBLEM—ON THE JOB FOR CHAPTER 10

SANCHEZ COMPUTER CENTER
GENERAL JOURNAL

PAGE 7

Date	Account Titles and Description	PR	Dr.	Cr.

PARTIAL GENERAL LEDGER

CASH   ACCOUNT NO. 1000

Date		Explanation	Post Ref.	Debit	Credit	Balance Debit	Balance Credit
2/1	1X	Balance forward	✔			15 1 6 6 65	

SUPPLIES   ACCOUNT NO. 1030

Date		Explanation	Post Ref.	Debit	Credit	Balance Debit	Balance Credit
2/1	1X	Balance forward	✔			9 0 00	

MERCHANDISE INVENTORY   ACCOUNT NO. 1040

Date		Explanation	Post Ref.	Debit	Credit	Balance Debit	Balance Credit

PREPAID RENT   ACCOUNT NO. 1025

Date		Explanation	Post Ref.	Debit	Credit	Balance	
						Debit	Credit
2/1	1X	Balance forward	✔			1 6 0 0 00	

ACCOUNTS PAYABLE   ACCOUNT NO. 2000

Date		Explanation	Post Ref.	Debit	Credit	Balance	
						Debit	Credit
2/1	1X	Balance forward	✔				2 0 5 0 00

PURCHASES   ACCOUNT NO. 6000

Date		Explanation	Post Ref.	Debit	Credit	Balance	
						Debit	Credit

PURCHASE RETURNS AND ALLOWANCES   ACCOUNT NO. 6010

Date		Explanation	Post Ref.	Debit	Credit	Balance	
						Debit	Credit

PURCHASE DISCOUNTS   ACCOUNT NO. 6020

Date		Explanation	Post Ref.	Debit	Credit	Balance	
						Debit	Credit

SANCHEZ COMPUTER CENTER
SCHEDULE OF ACCOUNTS PAYABLE
2/28/1X

ACCOUNTS PAYABLE SUBSIDIARY LEDGER

NAME **MULTI SYSTEMS, INC.**   **# 6A3**

ADDRESS **1919 MORAN ST., ANAHEIM, CA 92606**

Date			Explanation	Post Ref.	Debit	Credit	Cr. Balance
2/1	1X		Balance forward	✔			4 5 0 00

NAME **OFFICE DEPOT**   **# 6A4**

ADDRESS **460 ESCONDIDO BLVD., ESCONDIDO, CA 92025**

Date			Explanation	Post Ref.	Debit	Credit	Cr. Balance
2/1	1X		Balance forward	✔			5 0 00

NAME   **SAN DIEGO ELECTRIC**   # 6A5

ADDRESS   **606 INDUSTRIAL ST., SAN DIEGO, CA 92121**

Date		Explanation	Post Ref.	Debit	Credit	Cr. Balance

NAME   **PAC BELL**   # 6A6

ADDRESS   **101 BELL AVE., SAN DIEGO, CA 92101**

Date		Explanation	Post Ref.	Debit	Credit	Cr. Balance
2/1	1X	Balance forward	✔			1 5 0 00

NAME   **COMPUTER CONNECTION**   # 6A7

ADDRESS   **1020 WIL LANE, LOS ANGELES, CA 92405**

Date		Explanation	Post Ref.	Debit	Credit	Cr. Balance

NAME	SYSTEM DESIGN FURNITURE						# 6A8				

ADDRESS   2070 FIRST ST., SAN DIEGO, CA 92101

Date		Explanation	Post Ref.	Debit	Credit	Cr. Balance
2/1	1X	Balance forward	✔			1 4 0 0 00

APPENDIX 10A
FORMS FOR CLASSROOM DEMONSTRATION PROBLEM — SPECIAL JOURNALS

J. LING CO.
SALES JOURNAL

PAGE 1

Date	Account Debited	Terms	Invoice No.	Post Ref.	Dr. Acc. Receivable Cr. Sales

CASH RECEIPTS JOURNAL

PAGE 1

Date	Cash Dr.	Sales Discounts Dr.	Accounts Receivable Cr.	Sales Cr.	Sundry Account Name	PR	Amount Cr.

PURCHASES JOURNAL

PAGE 1

Date	Account Credited	Terms	PR	Accounts Payable Cr.	Purchases Dr.	Sundry Dr. Account	PR	Amount

CASH PAYMENTS JOURNAL

PAGE 1

Date	Check No.	Accounts Debited	PR	Sundry Account Dr.	Accounts Payable Dr.	Purchases Discounts Cr.	Cash Cr.

DEMO DOC PROBLEM (CONTINUED)

GENERAL JOURNAL

Date	Account Titles and Description	PR	Dr.	Cr.

ACCOUNTS RECEIVABLE SUBSIDIARY LEDGER

NAME   BALDER CO.

ADDRESS   1 ROCK RD., DENVER, CO 66083

Date	Explanation	Post Ref.	Debit	Credit	Dr. Balance

NAME   LEWIS CO.

ADDRESS   15 SMITH AVE., REVERE, MA 01545

Date	Explanation	Post Ref.	Debit	Credit	Dr. Balance

DEMO DOC PROBLEM (CONCLUDED)

ACCOUNTS PAYABLE SUBSIDIARY LEDGER

NAME CASE CO.

ADDRESS 1 LONG RD., MARLBOROUGH, MA 01545

Date		Explanation	Post Ref.	Debit	Credit	Cr. Balance

NAME NOONE CO.

ADDRESS 11 MILL RD., MALDEN, OK 01143

Date		Explanation	Post Ref.	Debit	Credit	Cr. Balance

PARTIAL GENERAL LEDGER

Cash 111	Sales 410	Purchases Discounts 530

Accounts Receivable 112	Sales Returns & Allowances 420	Salaries Expense 610

Equipment 116	Sales Discount 430	

Accounts Payable 210	Purchases 510	

J. Ling, Capital 310	Purchases Returns & Allowances 520	

CHAPTER 10A APPENDIX FORMS

PROBLEM A-1

(1, 2)

FOOD.COM
SALES JOURNAL

PAGE 1

Date	Account Debited	Invoice No.	PR	Accounts Receivable Dr.	Pizza Sales Cr.	Grocery Sales Cr.

(1, 2)

FOOD.COM
GENERAL JOURNAL

PAGE 1

Date	Account Titles and Description	PR	Dr.	Cr.

PROBLEM A-1 (CONTINUED)

ACCOUNTS RECEIVABLE SUBSIDIARY LEDGER

NAME   DUNCAN CO.

ADDRESS   942 MOSE ST., REVERE, MA 01938

Date	Explanation	Post Ref.	Debit	Credit	Dr. Balance

NAME   LONG CO.

ADDRESS   8 JOSS AVE., LYNN, MA 01947

Date	Explanation	Post Ref.	Debit	Credit	Dr. Balance

NAME   SUE MOORE CO.

ADDRESS   10 LOST RD., TOPSFIELD, MA 01998

Date	Explanation	Post Ref.	Debit	Credit	Dr. Balance

PROBLEM A-1 (CONTINUED)

FOOD.COM
GENERAL LEDGER

ACCOUNTS RECEIVABLE   **ACCOUNT NO. 112**

Date		Explanation	Post Ref.	Debit	Credit	Balance Debit	Balance Credit

PIZZA SALES   **ACCOUNT NO. 410**

Date		Explanation	Post Ref.	Debit	Credit	Balance Debit	Balance Credit

GROCERY SALES   **ACCOUNT NO. 411**

Date		Explanation	Post Ref.	Debit	Credit	Balance Debit	Balance Credit

SALES RETURNS AND ALLOWANCES   **ACCOUNT NO. 412**

Date		Explanation	Post Ref.	Debit	Credit	Balance Debit	Balance Credit

PROBLEM A-1 (CONCLUDED)

FOOD.COM
SCHEDULE OF ACCOUNTS RECEIVABLE
JUNE 30, 201X

PROBLEM A-2

(1, 2)

TED'S AUTO SUPPLY
SALES JOURNAL

PAGE 4

Date	Customer's Name Account Receivable	Invoice No.	PR	Accounts Receivable Dr.	Sales Tax Payable Cr.	Auto Parts Sales Cr.

PROBLEM A-2 (CONTINUED)

(1,2)

TED'S AUTO SUPPLY
GENERAL JOURNAL

PAGE 2

Date		Account Titles and Description	PR		Dr.		Cr.	

PROBLEM A-2 (CONTINUED)

ACCOUNTS RECEIVABLE SUBSIDIARY LEDGER

NAME   **LANCE CORNER**

ADDRESS   **9 ROE ST., BARTLETT, NH 01382**

Date 201X		Explanation	Post Ref.	Debit	Credit	Dr. Balance
Nov	1	Balance	✔			4 0 0 00

NAME   **J. SETH**

ADDRESS   **22 REESE ST., LACONIA, NH 04321**

Date 201X		Explanation	Post Ref.	Debit	Credit	Dr. Balance
Nov	1	Balance	✔			2 0 0 00

NAME   **R. VOLAN**

ADDRESS   **12 ASTER RD., MERRIMACK, NH 02134**

Date 201X		Explanation	Post Ref.	Debit	Credit	Dr. Balance
Nov	1	Balance	✔			1 0 0 0 00

PROBLEM A-2 (CONTINUED)

TED'S AUTO SUPPLY
GENERAL JOURNAL

ACCOUNTS RECEIVABLE ACCOUNT NO. 110

Date 201X		Explanation	Post Ref.	Debit	Credit	Balance Debit	Balance Credit
Nov	1	Balance	✔			1 6 0 0 00	

SALES TAX PAYABLE ACCOUNT NO. 210

Date 201X		Explanation	Post Ref.	Debit	Credit	Balance Debit	Balance Credit
Nov	1	Balance	✔				1 6 0 0 00

AUTO PARTS SALES ACCOUNT NO. 410

Date	Explanation	Post Ref.	Debit	Credit	Balance Debit	Balance Credit

SALES RETURNS AND ALLOWANCES ACCOUNT NO. 420

Date	Explanation	Post Ref.	Debit	Credit	Balance Debit	Balance Credit

PROBLEM A-2 (CONCLUDED)

(3)

TED'S AUTO SUPPLY
SCHEDULE OF ACCOUNTS RECEIVABLE
NOVEMBER 30, 201X

PROBLEM A-3

SKATES.COM
PURCHASES JOURNAL

Date	Account Credited	Date of Invoice	Inv. No.	Terms	PR	Accounts Payable Cr.	Purchases Dr.	Sundry Dr.		
								Account	PR	Amount

PROBLEM A-3 (CONTINUED)

ACCOUNTS PAYABLE SUBSIDIARY LEDGER

NAME MAIL.COM

ADDRESS 12 SMITH ST., DEARBORN, MI 09113

Date	Explanation	Post Ref.	Debit	Credit	Cr. Balance

NAME NORTON CO.

ADDRESS 1 RANTOUL RD., CHARLOTTE, NC 01114

Date	Explanation	Post Ref.	Debit	Credit	Cr. Balance

NAME ROLO CO.

ADDRESS 2 WEST RD., LYNN, MA 01471

Date	Explanation	Post Ref.	Debit	Credit	Cr. Balance

PARTIAL GENERAL LEDGER

STORE SUPPLIES   **ACCOUNT NO. 115**

Date	Explanation	Post Ref.	Debit	Credit	Balance Debit	Balance Credit

PROBLEM A-3 (CONCLUDED)

STORE EQUIPMENT   **ACCOUNT NO. 121**

Date	Explanation	Post Ref.	Debit	Credit	Balance Debit	Balance Credit

ACCOUNTS PAYABLE   **ACCOUNT NO. 210**

Date	Explanation	Post Ref.	Debit	Credit	Balance Debit	Balance Credit

PURCHASES   **ACCOUNT NO. 510**

Date	Explanation	Post Ref.	Debit	Credit	Balance Debit	Balance Credit

PROBLEM A-4

MABEL'S NATURAL FOOD STORE
PURCHASES JOURNAL

PAGE 10

Date	Account Credited	Date of Invoice	Inv. No.	Terms	PR	Accounts Payable Cr.	Purchases Dr.	Store Supplies Dr.	Account	PR	Amount

Sundry Dr.

PROBLEM A-4 (CONTINUED)

ACCOUNTS PAYABLE SUBSIDIARY LEDGER

NAME   ATON CO.

ADDRESS   11 LYNNWAY AVE., NEWPORT, RI 03112

Date 201X		Explanation	Post Ref.	Debit	Credit	Cr. Balance
May	1	Balance	✔			4 0 0 00

NAME   BROWARD CO.

ADDRESS   21 RIVER ST., ANAHEIM, CA 43110

Date 201X		Explanation	Post Ref.	Debit	Credit	Cr. Balance
May	1	Balance	✔			6 0 0 00

NAME   MIDDEN CO.

ADDRESS   10 ASTER RD., DUBUQUE, IA 80021

Date 201X		Explanation	Post Ref.	Debit	Credit	Cr. Balance
May	1	Balance	✔			1 2 0 0 00

NAME   RELAR CO.

ADDRESS   22 GERALD RD., SMITH, CO 43138

Date 201X		Explanation	Post Ref.	Debit	Credit	Cr. Balance
May	1	Balance	✔			5 0 0 00

PROBLEM A-4 (CONTINUED)

PARTIAL GENERAL LEDGER

STORE SUPPLIES   ACCOUNT NO. 110

Date	Explanation	Post Ref.	Debit	Credit	Balance Debit	Balance Credit

OFFICE EQUIPMENT   ACCOUNT NO. 120

Date	Explanation	Post Ref.	Debit	Credit	Balance Debit	Balance Credit

ACCOUNTS PAYABLE   ACCOUNT NO. 210

Date 201X	Explanation	Post Ref.	Debit	Credit	Balance Debit	Balance Credit
May 1	Balance	✔				2 7 0 0 00

PURCHASES   ACCOUNT NO. 510

Date 201X	Explanation	Post Ref.	Debit	Credit	Balance Debit	Balance Credit
May 1	Balance	✔			16 7 0 0 00	

PROBLEM A-4 (CONCLUDED)

PURCHASES RETURNS AND ALLOWANCES   ACCOUNT NO. 512

Date		Explanation	Post Ref.	Debit	Credit	Balance Debit	Balance Credit

GENERAL JOURNAL   PAGE 2

Date		Account Titles and Description	PR	Dr.	Cr.

MABEL'S NATURAL FOOD STORE
SCHEDULE OF ACCOUNTS PAYABLE
MAY 31, 201X

PROBLEM A-5

(1, 3)

ABBY'S TOY HOUSE
PURCHASES JOURNAL

PAGE 1

Date	Account Credited	Date of Inv.	Inv. No.	Terms	PR	Accounts Payable Cr.	Toy Purchases Dr.	Accounts	PR	Amount

Sundry Dr.

PROBLEM A-5 (CONTINUED)

ABBY'S TOY HOUSE
CASH RECEIPTS JOURNAL

PAGE 1

Date	Cash Dr.	Sales Discounts Dr.	Accounts Receivable Cr.	Toy Sales Cr.	Sundry Account	PR	Amount Cr.

PROBLEM A-5 (CONTINUED)

ABBY'S TOY HOUSE
CASH PAYMENTS JOURNAL

PAGE 1

Date	Check No.	Account Debited	PR	Sundry Dr.	Accounts Payable Dr.	Purchases Discount Cr.	Cash Cr.

PROBLEM A-5 (CONTINUED)

**ABBY'S TOY HOUSE
SALES JOURNAL
MARCH 31, 201X**

PAGE 1

Date	Account Debited	Invoice No.	Terms	PR	Accounts Rec. – Dr. Toy Sales – Cr.

**ABBY'S TOY HOUSE
GENERAL JOURNAL
MARCH 31, 201X**

PAGE 1

Date	Account Titles and Description	PR	Dr.	Cr.

PROBLEM A-5 (CONTINUED)

(2)   **ACCOUNTS PAYABLE SUBSIDIARY LEDGER**

NAME   MINNIE KATZ

ADDRESS   87 GARFIELD AVE., REVERE, MA 01245

Date	Explanation	Post Ref.	Debit	Credit	Cr. Balance

NAME   SAM KATZ GARAGE

ADDRESS   22 REGIS RD., BOSTON, MA 01950

Date	Explanation	Post Ref.	Debit	Credit	Cr. Balance

NAME   EARL MILLER CO.

ADDRESS   22 RETTER ST., SAN DIEGO, CA 01211

Date	Explanation	Post Ref.	Debit	Credit	Cr. Balance

NAME   WOODY SMITH

ADDRESS   2 SPRING ST., WEERS, ND 02118

Date	Explanation	Post Ref.	Debit	Credit	Cr. Balance

PROBLEM A-5 (CONTINUED)

ACCOUNTS RECEIVABLE SUBSIDIARY LEDGER

NAME   BILL BURTON

ADDRESS   24 RYAN RD., BUIKE, OH 02183

Date	Explanation	Post Ref.	Debit	Credit	Dr. Balance

NAME   BONNIE FLOW CO.

ADDRESS   2 SMITH RD., DALLAS, TX 22210

Date	Explanation	Post Ref.	Debit	Credit	Dr. Balance

NAME   JIM REX

ADDRESS   1 SCHOOL ST., CLEVELAND, OH 22441

Date	Explanation	Post Ref.	Debit	Credit	Dr. Balance

PROBLEM A-5 (CONTINUED)

NAME   AMY ROSE

ADDRESS   18 VEEK RD., CHESTER, CT 80111

Date		Explanation	Post Ref.	Debit	Credit	Dr. Balance

GENERAL LEDGER

CASH   ACCOUNT NO. 110

Date		Explanation	Post Ref.	Debit	Credit	Balance Debit	Balance Credit

ACCOUNTS RECEIVABLE   ACCOUNT NO. 112

Date		Explanation	Post Ref.	Debit	Credit	Balance Debit	Balance Credit

PREPAID RENT   ACCOUNT NO. 114

Date		Explanation	Post Ref.	Debit	Credit	Balance Debit	Balance Credit

PROBLEM A-5 (CONTINUED)

DELIVERY TRUCK   **ACCOUNT NO. 121**

Date		Explanation	Post Ref.	Debit	Credit	Balance	
						Debit	Credit

ACCOUNTS PAYABLE   **ACCOUNT NO. 210**

Date		Explanation	Post Ref.	Debit	Credit	Balance	
						Debit	Credit

A. ELLEN, CAPITAL   **ACCOUNT NO. 310**

Date		Explanation	Post Ref.	Debit	Credit	Balance	
						Debit	Credit

TOY SALES   **ACCOUNT NO. 410**

Date		Explanation	Post Ref.	Debit	Credit	Balance	
						Debit	Credit

PROBLEM A-5 (CONTINUED)

SALES RETURNS AND ALLOWANCES — ACCOUNT NO. 412

Date	Explanation	Post Ref.	Debit	Credit	Balance Debit	Balance Credit

SALES DISCOUNTS — ACCOUNT NO. 414

Date	Explanation	Post Ref.	Debit	Credit	Balance Debit	Balance Credit

TOY PURCHASES — ACCOUNT NO. 510

Date	Explanation	Post Ref.	Debit	Credit	Balance Debit	Balance Credit

PURCHASES RETURNS AND ALLOWANCES — ACCOUNT NO. 512

Date	Explanation	Post Ref.	Debit	Credit	Balance Debit	Balance Credit

PROBLEM A-5 (CONTINUED)

PURCHASES DISCOUNT   **ACCOUNT NO. 514**

Date		Explanation	Post Ref.	Debit	Credit	Balance Debit	Balance Credit

SALARIES EXPENSE   **ACCOUNT NO. 610**

Date		Explanation	Post Ref.	Debit	Credit	Balance Debit	Balance Credit

CLEANING EXPENSE   **ACCOUNT NO. 612**

Date		Explanation	Post Ref.	Debit	Credit	Balance Debit	Balance Credit

PROBLEM A-5 (CONCLUDED)

(4)

ABBY'S TOY HOUSE
SCHEDULE OF ACCOUNTS RECEIVABLE
MARCH 31, 201X

(4)

ABBY'S TOY HOUSE
SCHEDULE OF ACCOUNTS PAYABLE
MARCH 31, 201X

11

Preparing a Worksheet for a Merchandise Company

INSTANT REPLAY: SELF-REVIEW QUIZ 11-1

INSTANT REPLAY: SELF-REVIEW QUIZ 11-2

Use one of the blank fold-out worksheets that accompanied your textbook.

CHAPTER 11
CONCEPT CHECK

1.														
2.														

3. A. _____   E. _____

B. _____   F. _____

C. _____

D. _____

4. _____

_____

_____

_____

_____

_____

_____

5.

A. _____ B. _____ C. _____ D. _____ E. _____ F. _____

FORMS FOR EXERCISES A OR B

11A-1 OR 11B-1.

A. _____
B. _____
C. _____
D. _____
E. _____
F. _____
G. _____
H. _____

11A-2 OR 11B-2.

A. _____
_____
_____

B. _____
_____
_____

C. _____
_____
_____

D. _____
_____
_____

11A-3 OR 11B-3.

Accounts Affected	Category	↑↓	Rules

11A-4 OR 11B-4.

A. _____
B. _____
C. _____

11A-5 OR 11B-5.

Use one of the blank fold-out worksheets that accompanied your textbook.

END OF CHAPTER PROBLEMS

PROBLEM 11A-1 OR PROBLEM 11B-1

	A.	
	B.	
	C.	
	D.	

PROBLEM 11A-2 OR PROBLEM 11B-2;
PROBLEM 11A-3 OR PROBLEM 11B-3;
PROBLEM 11A-4 OR PROBLEM 11B-4

Use blank fold-out worksheets that accompanied your textbook.

CHAPTER 11
SUMMARY PRACTICE TEST:
PREPARING A WORKSHEET
FOR A MERCHANDISE COMPANY

Part I Instructions

Fill in the blank(s) to complete the statement.

1. The _____ _____ system keeps a continual track of the quantity and cost of the inventory on hand.

2. In the periodic inventory system, new inventories bought is recorded in the _____ account.

3. A continuous record of inventory is kept in a(n) _____ _____ system.

4. When using the periodic system, _____ _____ will remain unchanged.

5. _____ _____ represents a liability on the balance sheet and records money received for a sale or service not yet performed.

6. Freight-in is _____ to the cost of goods sold.

7. Net Sales less Cost of Goods Sold equals _____ _____.

8. _____ _____ equals Gross Sales less Sales Discounts and Sales Returns and Allowances.

9. Net Purchases equals Purchases less _____ _____ and _____ _____ _____ _____.

10. A(n) _____ _____ helps calculate ending inventory.

11. Ending inventory is _____ from the cost of goods available for sale.

12. Net purchases are _____ to Beginning Inventory to get the cost of goods available for sale.

13. Gross Profit less _____ equals Net Income.

14. Purchase discounts _____ the total cost of merchandise sold.

15. Beginning inventory at the end of the period is assumed to be _____, and thus a _____.

16. The ending inventory of one period becomes the _____ _____ next period.

17. Ending inventory represents goods not _____.

18. The inventory account is _____ at the end of the period.

19. Purchases are increased by a(n) _____.

20. Sales returns and allowances are used in calculating _____ _____.

21. Beginning Inventory plus Net Purchases equals _____ _____ _____ _____ _____ _____.

22. Beginning Inventory and Ending Inventory are never _____ on the worksheet.

Part II Instructions

Answer true or false to the following statements.

1. Unearned Revenue is a liability.
2. Perpetual inventory keeps a continuous record of inventory.
3. Purchases increase cost of goods sold.
4. Freight-in is added to cost of goods sold.
5. Figures for Beginning and Ending Inventory are combined on the worksheet.
6. A periodic system is used by companies with low volume and high unit prices.
7. Merchandise Inventory is an asset.
8. Unearned Revenue is a liability on the income statement.
9. Inventory is always taken 10 times per year.
10. Purchases replace ending inventory in a periodic system.
11. A trial balance may be placed directly on a worksheet.
12. The adjustment process updates the inventory account.
13. A post-closing trial balance has no temporary accounts.
14. Sales Discounts is a permanent account.
15. Gross sales are located on the balance sheet.
16. The Sales Returns and Allowances account has a normal balance of a credit.
17. Ending inventory of one period is the beginning inventory of the following period.
18. Net income always means cash.
19. Ending inventory increases cost of goods sold.
20. Net purchases is always the same as total purchases.
21. Gross profit plus expenses equals net income.
22. Unearned Storage Fees is a liability.
23. Merchandise inventory that is sold is assumed to be a cost.
24. Accumulated Depreciation is increased by a debit.
25. Merchandise Inventory can never be listed on a trial balance.
26. Ending Merchandise Inventory can only be found on a balance sheet.
27. The amount of rent expired is used in the adjustment process.
28. Adjustments help update individual ledger accounts.
29. Purchases Returns and Allowances is found on a balance sheet.
30. Beginning Merchandise Inventory found on the balance sheet from the prior period will also be placed in the cost of goods sold section of the balance sheet.
31. Sales always means cash received.
32. Ending Merchandise Inventory of the current period is found only on the balance sheet.
33. Purchases adds to the cost of goods sold.
34. Purchases discounts reduce the cost of purchases on the balance sheet.
35. Beginning inventory can never be assumed sold by the end of a period.

36. Ending inventory in one period becomes beginning inventory for the next two periods.

37. The ending inventory may be calculated from an inventory sheet.

38. Income Summary is used in the adjustment of merchandise inventory.

39. Ending inventory not sold is only placed in the credit column of the balance sheet section on the worksheet.

40. Purchases Discount is recorded in the credit column of the income statement section on the worksheet.

41. Gross profit and net income mean the same.

42. All companies must give sales discounts.

43. A merchandise company does not need a cost of goods sold section on the income statement.

44. Cost of goods available to sell less ending inventory equals cost of goods not sold.

SOLUTIONS TO SUMMARY PRACTICE TEST

Part I

1. perpetual inventory
2. Purchases
3. perpetual inventory
4. beginning inventory
5. Unearned Revenue
6. added
7. Gross Profit
8. Net sales
9. Purchases Discounts, Purchases Returns and Allowances
10. Inventory sheet (record)
11. subtracted
12. added
13. Expenses
14. reduce
15. sold, cost
16. begining inventory
17. sold
18. adjusted
19. debit
20. net sales
21. Cost of Goods Available for Sale
22. combined

Part II

1. true	**12.** true	**23.** true	**34.** false
2. true	**13.** true	**24.** false	**35.** false
3. true	**14.** false	**25.** false	**36.** false
4. true	**15.** false	**26.** false	**37.** true
5. false	**16.** false	**27.** true	**38.** true
6. false	**17.** true	**28.** true	**39.** false
7. true	**18.** false	**29.** false	**40.** true
8. false	**19.** false	**30.** false	**41.** false
9. false	**20.** false	**31.** false	**42.** false
10. false	**21.** false	**32.** false	**43.** false
11. true	**22.** true	**33.** true	**44.** false

CONTINUING PROBLEM—ON THE JOB FOR CHAPTER 11

Use the blank fold-out worksheet that accompanied your textbook.

12

COMPLETION OF THE ACCOUNTING CYCLE FOR A MERCHANDISE COMPANY

INSTANT REPLAY: SELF-REVIEW QUIZ 12-1

(1)

_____

_____

(2)

INSTANT REPLAY: SELF-REVIEW QUIZ 12-2

GENERAL JOURNAL   PAGE 2

Date	Account Titles and Description		PR	Dr	Cr.

INSTANT REPLAY: SELF-REVIEW QUIZ 12-3

Situation 1

Situation 2

Situation 3

CHAPTER 12
CONCEPT CHECK

1. _____
_____
_____
_____

2. _____
_____
_____
_____
_____

3. _____
_____
_____
_____
_____

4. A. _____   F. _____
B. _____   G. _____
C. _____   H. _____
D. _____   I. _____
E. _____   J. _____

5.

FORMS FOR EXERCISES A or B

12A-1 OR 12B-1.

COST OF GOODS SOLD

Merchandise Inv. 12/01/1X _____

Purchases _____

Less: Purchases Disc. _____

        Purch. R. & A. _____

_____

 Net Purchases _____

       Add: Freight-in _____

Net Cost of Purchases _____

Cost of Goods Available for Sale _____

Less: Merchandise Inv. 12/31/1X _____

       Cost of Goods Sold _____

12A-2 OR 12B-2.

A. _____

B. _____

C. _____

D. _____

E. _____

F. _____

G. _____

12A-3 OR 12B-3.

EXERCISES (CONCLUDED)

12A-4 OR 12B-4.

G. JACKSON
PARTIAL BALANCE SHEET
DECEMBER 31, 201X

12A-5 OR 12B-5.

(A)

Salaries Expense	Salaries Payable

(B)

Salaries Expense	Salaries Expense

(C)

Salaries Expense	Cash

END OF CHAPTER PROBLEMS

PROBLEM 12A-1 OR PROBLEM 12B-1

ROSE CO.
INCOME STATEMENT
FOR YEAR ENDED DECEMBER 31, 201X

PROBLEM 12A-2 OR PROBLEM 12B-2

JOHN'S CO.
STATEMENT OF OWNER'S EQUITY
FOR MONTH ENDED DECEMBER 31, 201X

PROBLEM 12A-2 OR PROBLEM 12B-2 (CONCLUDED)

JOHN'S CO.
BALANCE SHEET
DECEMBER 31, 201X

PROBLEM 12A-3 OR PROBLEM 12B-3

Use one of the blank fold-out worksheets that accompanied your textbook.

JOE'S SUPPLIES
INCOME STATEMENT
FOR YEAR ENDED DECEMBER 31, 201X

PROBLEM 12A-3 OR PROBLEM 12B-3 (CONTINUED)

JOE'S SUPPLIES
STATEMENT OF OWNER'S EQUITY
FOR YEAR ENDED DECEMBER 31, 201X

PROBLEM 12A-3 OR PROBLEM 12B-3 (CONTINUED)

JOE'S SUPPLIES
BALANCE SHEET
DECEMBER 31, 201X

PROBLEM 12A-3 OR PROBLEM 12B-3 (CONTINUED)

GENERAL JOURNAL

PAGE 2

Date		Account Titles and Description	PR		Dr.		Cr.	

PROBLEM 12A-3 OR PROBLEM 12B-3 (CONCLUDED)

GENERAL JOURNAL

PAGE 3

Date		Account Titles and Description	PR		Dr.			Cr.		

PROBLEM 12A-4 OR PROBLEM 12B-4

Use one of the blank fold-out worksheets that accompanied your textbook.

CROSS LUMBER
INCOME STATEMENT
FOR YEAR ENDED DECEMBER 31, 201X

PROBLEM 12A-4 OR PROBLEM 12B-4 (CONTINUED)

Use one of the blank fold-out worksheets that accompanied your textbook.

CROSS LUMBER
STATEMENT OF OWNER'S EQUITY
FOR YEAR ENDED DECEMBER 31, 201X

PROBLEM 12A-4 OR PROBLEM 12B-4 (CONTINUED)

CROSS LUMBER
BALANCE SHEET
DECEMBER 31, 201X

PROBLEM 12A-4 OR PROBLEM 12B-4 (CONTINUED)

GENERAL JOURNAL

Date	Account Titles and Description	PR	Dr.	Cr.

PROBLEM 12A-4 OR PROBLEM 12B-4 (CONTINUED)

CROSS LUMBER
GENERAL LEDGER

CASH   **ACCOUNT NO. 110**

Date	Explanation	Post Ref.	Debit	Credit	Balance Debit	Balance Credit

ACCOUNTS RECEIVABLE   **ACCOUNT NO. 111**

Date	Explanation	Post Ref.	Debit	Credit	Balance Debit	Balance Credit

MERCHANDISE INVENTORY   **ACCOUNT NO. 112**

Date	Explanation	Post Ref.	Debit	Credit	Balance Debit	Balance Credit

LUMBER SUPPLIES   **ACCOUNT NO. 113**

Date	Explanation	Post Ref.	Debit	Credit	Balance Debit	Balance Credit

PROBLEM 12A-4 OR PROBLEM 12B-4 (CONTINUED)

PREPAID INSURANCE   ACCOUNT NO. 114

Date	Explanation	Post Ref.	Debit	Credit	Balance Debit	Balance Credit

LUMBER EQUIPMENT   ACCOUNT NO. 121

Date	Explanation	Post Ref.	Debit	Credit	Balance Debit	Balance Credit

ACCUMULATED DEPRECIATION, LUMBER EQUIPMENT   ACCOUNT NO. 122

Date	Explanation	Post Ref.	Debit	Credit	Balance Debit	Balance Credit

ACCOUNTS PAYABLE   ACCOUNT NO. 220

Date	Explanation	Post Ref.	Debit	Credit	Balance Debit	Balance Credit

WAGES PAYABLE   ACCOUNT NO. 221

Date	Explanation	Post Ref.	Debit	Credit	Balance Debit	Balance Credit

PROBLEM 12A-4 OR PROBLEM 12B-4 (CONTINUED)

J. CROSS, CAPITAL   ACCOUNT NO. 330

Date	Explanation	Post Ref.	Debit	Credit	Balance Debit	Balance Credit

J. CROSS, WITHDRAWALS   ACCOUNT NO. 331

Date	Explanation	Post Ref.	Debit	Credit	Balance Debit	Balance Credit

INCOME SUMMARY   ACCOUNT NO. 332

Date	Explanation	Post Ref.	Debit	Credit	Balance Debit	Balance Credit

SALES   ACCOUNT NO. 440

Date	Explanation	Post Ref.	Debit	Credit	Balance Debit	Balance Credit

SALES RETURNS AND ALLOWANCES   ACCOUNT NO. 441

Date	Explanation	Post Ref.	Debit	Credit	Balance Debit	Balance Credit

PROBLEM 12A-4 OR PROBLEM 12B-4 (CONTINUED)

PURCHASES   ACCOUNT NO. 550

Date	Explanation	Post Ref.	Debit	Credit	Balance Debit	Credit

PURCHASES DISCOUNT   ACCOUNT NO. 551

Date	Explanation	Post Ref.	Debit	Credit	Balance Debit	Credit

PURCHASES RETURNS AND ALLOWANCES   ACCOUNT NO. 552

Date	Explanation	Post Ref.	Debit	Credit	Balance Debit	Credit

WAGES EXPENSE   ACCOUNT NO. 660

Date	Explanation	Post Ref.	Debit	Credit	Balance Debit	Credit

ADVERTISING EXPENSE   ACCOUNT NO. 661

Date	Explanation	Post Ref.	Debit	Credit	Balance Debit	Credit

PROBLEM 12A-4 OR PROBLEM 12B-4 (CONTINUED)

RENT EXPENSE   ACCOUNT NO. 662

Date	Explanation	Post Ref.	Debit	Credit	Balance Debit	Balance Credit

DEPRECIATION EXPENSE, LUMBER EQUIPMENT   ACCOUNT NO. 663

Date	Explanation	Post Ref.	Debit	Credit	Balance Debit	Balance Credit

LUMBER SUPPLIES EXPENSE   ACCOUNT NO. 664

Date	Explanation	Post Ref.	Debit	Credit	Balance Debit	Balance Credit

INSURANCE EXPENSE   ACCOUNT NO. 665

Date	Explanation	Post Ref.	Debit	Credit	Balance Debit	Balance Credit

PROBLEM 12A-4 OR PROBLEM 12B-4 (CONCLUDED)

CROSS LUMBER
POST-CLOSING TRIAL BALANCE
DECEMBER 31, 201X

	Dr.	Cr.

CHAPTER 12
SUMMARY PRACTICE TEST:
COMPLETION OF THE ACCOUNTING
CYCLE FOR A MERCHANDISE COMPANY

Part I Instructions

Fill in the blank(s) to complete the statement.

1. There are no debits or credits on _____ _____.

2. The formal income statement uses _____ _____ figures for inventory.

3. The gross profit figure _____ (is/is not) found on the worksheet.

4. _____ expenses are related to the general activity.

5. _____ _____ are related to the administrative function.

6. _____ _____ could be broken down into selling and administrative expenses.

7. The _____ figure for capital is not found on the worksheet.

8. _____ _____ are cash or other assets that will be converted into cash during the normal operating cycle of the company or one year, whichever is longer.

9. _____ and _____ are long-lived assets used for the production or sale of other assets or services.

10. Debts or obligations that are to be paid with current assets within one year or one operating cycle are called _____ _____.

11. Mortgage Payable is an example of a(n) _____ _____ _____.

12. Ending merchandise inventory is a(n) _____ _____.

13. By the adjusting process, the beginning inventory of the period is transferred to _____ _____.

14. The _____ _____ _____ _____ contains no temporary accounts.

15. A reversing entry involves certain _____ entries.

16. Reversing entries are used only if assets are _____ and have no previous balance and liabilities are _____ and have no balance.

Part II Instructions

Match the term in the last column to the definition, example, or phrase in the right column. Be sure to use a letter only once.

d	**1.** EXAMPLE: Computer Equipment	a.	Subtotaling
_____	**2.** Net Sales-Cost of Goods Sold	b.	Unearned Revenue
_____	**3.** Operating Cycle	c.	Current asset
_____	**4.** Inside Columns of Financial Reports	d.	Plant and Equipment
_____	**5.** Gross Profit-Operating Expenses	e.	Reversing Entry
_____	**6.** Operating Expenses	f.	Time Period
_____	**7.** Temporary Account	g.	Net Income
_____	**8.** OASDI	h.	Current Liability
_____	**9.** Result of an adjusting entry	i.	When earned reduced by a debit
_____	**10.** Petty Cash	j.	Gross Profit
_____	**11.** An asset that is adjsuted	k.	Merchandise Inventory
_____	**12.** Ending Capital	l.	Debit Balance
_____	**13.** A Liability showing revenue no earned	m.	Not found on worksheet
_____	**14.** Unearned training fees	n.	Income Summary
		o.	Selling and Administrative

Part III Instructions

Answer true or false to the following statements.

1. A balance sheet records all revenue.
2. Cost of goods sold contains only ending inventory.
3. Net sales less cost of goods sold equals gross profit.
4. Operating expenses can only be administrative.
5. Supplies is part of Plant and Equipment.
6. Unearned Rent is an asset.
7. An operating cycle of a business must be one year.
8. Accumulated Depreciation is a current asset.
9. Long-term liabilities are due within one year.
10. Merchandise Inventory is a temporary account.
11. The normal balance of merchandise inventory is a debit.
12. The post-closing trial balance will not contain any unearned revenue accounts.
13. Ending inventory is closed directly to Capital.
14. Reversing entries cannot be applied to all adjustments.
15. Reversing entries are optional at the end of each month before the close of the year.
16. Reversing entries switch closing entries on the first day of the new period.
17. An adjusting entry with an asset decreasing with no prevoius balance cannot be reversed.
18. Closing entries will update the merchandise inventory account.
19. Beginning merchandise inventory of a period is assumed sold by the end of the period.
20. An adjusting entry for Accrued Wages can be reversed.

CHAPTER 12
SOLUTIONS TO SUMMARY PRACTICE TEST

Part I

1. financial reports
2. two separate
3. is not
4. General
5. Administrative expenses
6. Operating expenses
7. ending
8. Current assets
9. Plant, Equipment
10. current liabilities
11. long-term liability
12. permanent account
13. Income Summary
14. post-closing trial balance
15. adjusting
16. increasing, increasing

Part II

1. d
2. j
3. f
4. a
5. g
6. o
7. n
8. h
9. e
10. l
11. k
12. m
13. b
14. i

Part III

1. false
2. false
3. true
4. false
5. false
6. false
7. false
8. false
9. false
10. false
11. true
12. false
13. false
14. true
15. false
16. false
17. true
18. false
19. true
20. true

CONTINUING PROBLEM—ON THE JOB FOR CHAPTER 12

SANCHEZ COMPUTER CENTER
GENERAL JOURNAL

Date		Account Titles and Description	PR		Dr.				Cr.		

SANCHEZ COMPUTER CENTER
GENERAL LEDGER

CASH   **ACCOUNT NO. 1000**

Date		Explanation	Post Ref.	Debit	Credit	Balance	
						Debit	Credit
3/1	1X	Balance forward	✔			13 4 1 6 64	

PETTY CASH   **ACCOUNT NO. 1010**

Date		Explanation	Post Ref.	Debit	Credit	Balance	
						Debit	Credit
3/1	1X	Balance forward	✔			1 0 0 00	

ACCOUNTS RECEIVABLE   **ACCOUNT NO. 1020**

Date		Explanation	Post Ref.	Debit	Credit	Balance	
						Debit	Credit
3/1	1X	Balance forward	✔			10 9 0 0 00	

PREPAID RENT   **ACCOUNT NO. 1025**

Date		Explanation	Post Ref.	Debit	Credit	Balance	
						Debit	Credit
3/1	1X	Balance forward	✔			2 8 0 0 00	

Name _____ Class _____ Date _____

SUPPLIES   ACCOUNT NO. 1030

Date		Explanation	Post Ref.	Debit	Credit	Balance Debit	Balance Credit
3/1	1X	Balance forward	✔			3 9 0 00	

MERCHANDISE INVENTORY   ACCOUNT NO. 1040

Date		Explanation	Post Ref.	Debit	Credit	Balance Debit	Balance Credit

COMPUTER SHOP EQUIPMENT   ACCOUNT NO. 1080

Date		Explanation	Post Ref.	Debit	Credit	Balance Debit	Balance Credit
3/1	1X	Balance forward	✔			3 8 0 0	

ACCUMULATED DEPRECIATION, C.S. EQUIPMENT   ACCOUNT NO. 1081

Date		Explanation	Post Ref.	Debit	Credit	Balance Debit	Balance Credit
3/1	1X	Balance forward	✔				9 9 00

OFFICE EQUIPMENT   ACCOUNT NO. 1090

Date		Explanation	Post Ref.	Debit	Credit	Balance Debit	Balance Credit
3/1	1X	Balance forward	✔			1 0 5 0 00	

ACCUMULATED DEPRECIATION, OFFICE EQUIPMENT   ACCOUNT NO. 1091

Date		Explanation	Post Ref.	Debit	Credit	Balance Debit	Balance Credit
3/1	1X	Balance forward	✔				2 0 00

ACCOUNTS PAYABLE   ACCOUNT NO. 2000

Date		Explanation	Post Ref.	Debit	Credit	Balance Debit	Balance Credit
3/1	1X	Balance forward	✔				2 7 0 0 00

WAGES PAYABLE   ACCOUNT NO. 2010

Date		Explanation	Post Ref.	Debit	Credit	Balance Debit	Balance Credit

FICA OASDI PAYABLE   ACCOUNT NO. 2020

Date		Explanation	Post Ref.	Debit	Credit	Balance Debit	Balance Credit

FICA MEDICARE PAYABLE   ACCOUNT NO. 2030

Date		Explanation	Post Ref.	Debit	Credit	Balance Debit	Balance Credit

FIT PAYABLE   ACCOUNT NO. 2040

Date		Explanation	Post Ref.	Debit	Credit	Balance Debit	Balance Credit

SIT PAYABLE   ACCOUNT NO. 2050

Date		Explanation	Post Ref.	Debit	Credit	Balance Debit	Balance Credit

FUTA PAYABLE   ACCOUNT NO. 2060

Date		Explanation	Post Ref.	Debit	Credit	Balance Debit	Balance Credit

SUTA PAYABLE   ACCOUNT NO. 2070

Date		Explanation	Post Ref.	Debit	Credit	Balance Debit	Balance Credit

T. FREEDMAN, CAPITAL   ACCOUNT NO. 3000

Date		Explanation	Post Ref.	Debit	Credit	Balance Debit	Balance Credit
3/1	1X	Balance forward	✔				7 4 0 6 00

T. FREEDMAN WITHDRAWALS   ACCOUNT NO. 3010

Date		Explanation	Post Ref.	Debit	Credit	Balance	
						Debit	Credit
3/1	1X	Balance forward	✔			2 0 1 5 00	

INCOME SUMMARY   ACCOUNT NO. 3020

Date		Explanation	Post Ref.	Debit	Credit	Balance	
						Debit	Credit

SERVICE REVENUE   ACCOUNT NO. 4000

Date		Explanation	Post Ref.	Debit	Credit	Balance	
						Debit	Credit
3/1	1X	Balance forward	✔				18 5 0 0 00

SALES   ACCOUNT NO. 4010

Date		Explanation	Post Ref.	Debit	Credit	Balance	
						Debit	Credit
3/1	1X	Balance forward	✔				9 7 0 0 00

GENERAL LEDGER

SALES RETURNS AND ALLOWANCES   ACCOUNT NO. 4020

Date		Explanation	Post Ref.	Debit	Credit	Balance Debit	Balance Credit
3/1	1X	Balance forward	✔			4 0 0 00	

SALES DISCOUNTS   ACCOUNT NO. 4030

Date		Explanation	Post Ref.	Debit	Credit	Balance Debit	Balance Credit
3/1	1X	Balance forward	✔			2 2 0 00	

ADVERTISING EXPENSE   ACCOUNT NO. 5010

Date	Explanation	Post Ref.	Debit	Credit	Balance Debit	Balance Credit
	Balance forward					

RENT EXPENSE   ACCOUNT NO. 5020

Date	Explanation	Post Ref.	Debit	Credit	Balance Debit	Balance Credit

UTILITIES EXPENSE   ACCOUNT NO. 5030

Date	Explanation	Post Ref.	Debit	Credit	Balance Debit	Balance Credit
	Balance forward					

PHONE EXPENSE ACCOUNT NO. 5040

Date		Explanation	Post Ref.	Debit	Credit	Balance Debit	Balance Credit
3/1	1X	Balance forward	✔			1 5 0 00	

SUPPLIES EXPENSE ACCOUNT NO. 5050

Date		Explanation	Post Ref.	Debit	Credit	Balance Debit	Balance Credit
3/1	1X		✔			4 2 00	

INSURANCE EXPENSE ACCOUNT NO. 5060

Date		Explanation	Post Ref.	Debit	Credit	Balance Debit	Balance Credit

POSTAGE EXPENSE ACCOUNT NO. 5070

Date		Explanation	Post Ref.	Debit	Credit	Balance Debit	Balance Credit
3/1	1X	Balance forward	✔			2 5 00	

DEPRECIATION EXPENSE C.S. EQUIPMENT ACCOUNT NO. 5080

Date		Explanation	Post Ref.	Debit	Credit	Balance Debit	Balance Credit

DEPRECIATION EXPENSE OFFICE EQUIPMENT ACCOUNT NO. 5090

Date		Explanation	Post Ref.	Debit	Credit	Balance Debit	Balance Credit

MISCELLANEOUS EXPENSE ACCOUNT NO. 5100

Date		Explanation	Post Ref.	Debit	Credit	Balance Debit	Balance Credit
3/1	1X	Balance forward	✔			1 0 00	

WAGE EXPENSE ACCOUNT NO. 5110

Date		Explanation	Post Ref.	Debit	Credit	Balance Debit	Balance Credit
3/1	1X	Balance forward	✔			2 0 3 0 00	

PAYROLL TAX EXPENSE ACCOUNT NO. 5120

Date		Explanation	Post Ref.	Debit	Credit	Balance Debit	Balance Credit
3/1	1X	Balance forward	✔			2 2 6 36	

INTEREST EXPENSE ACCOUNT NO. 5130

Date		Explanation	Post Ref.	Debit	Credit	Balance Debit	Balance Credit

BAD DEBT EXPENSE   ACCOUNT NO. 5140

Date		Explanation	Post Ref.	Debit	Credit	Balance	
						Debit	Credit

PURCHASES   ACCOUNT NO. 6000

Date		Explanation	Post Ref.	Debit	Credit	Balance	
						Debit	Credit
3/1	1X	Balance forward	✔			9 5 0 00	

PURCHASE RETURNS AND ALLOWANCES   ACCOUNT NO. 6010

Date		Explanation	Post Ref.	Debit	Credit	Balance	
						Debit	Credit
3/1	1X	Balance forward	✔				1 0 0 00

PURCHASE DISCOUNTS   ACCOUNT NO. 6020

Date		Explanation	Post Ref.	Debit	Credit	Balance	
						Debit	Credit

FREIGHT IN   ACCOUNT NO. 6030

Date		Explanation	Post Ref.	Debit	Credit	Balance	
						Debit	Credit

SANCHEZ COMPUTER CENTER
INCOME STATEMENT
FOR THE SIX MONTHS ENDED MARCH 31, 201X

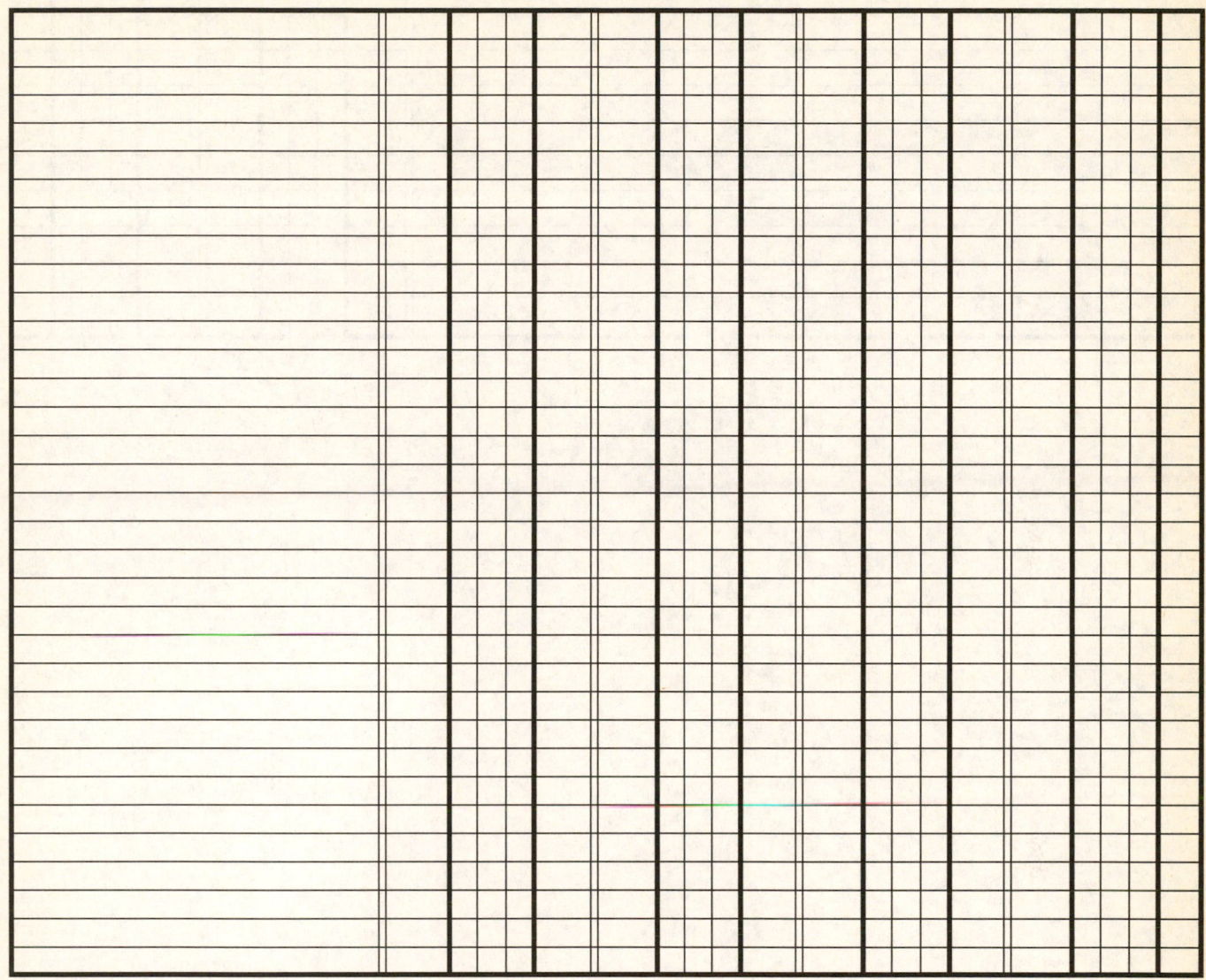

SANCHEZ COMPUTER CENTER
STATEMENT OF OWNER'S EQUITY
FOR THE SIX MONTHS ENDED MARCH 31, 201X

SANCHEZ COMPUTER CENTER
BALANCE SHEET
MARCH 31, 201X

MINI PRACTICE SET

THE CORNER DRESS SHOP
GENERAL JOURNAL   PAGE 4

Date	Account Titles and Description	PR	Dr.	Cr.

THE CORNER DRESS SHOP

Use a blank fold-out worksheet and a blank payroll register that accompanied your textbook.

MINI PRACTICE SET

Use the blank fold-out worksheets that accompanied your textbook.

THE CORNER DRESS SHOP
GENERAL JOURNAL

PAGE 5

Date		Account Titles and Description	PR	Dr.	Cr.

MINI PRACTICE SET

THE CORNER DRESS SHOP
GENERAL JOURNAL

Date		Account Titles and Description	PR	Dr.		Cr.	

MINI PRACTICE SET

THE CORNER DRESS SHOP
GENERAL JOURNAL

PAGE 7

Date	Account Titles and Description	PR	Dr.	Cr.

MINI PRACTICE SET

THE CORNER DRESS SHOP
GENERAL JOURNAL   PAGE 8

Date		Account Titles and Description	PR	Dr.	Cr.

MINI PRACTICE SET

THE CORNER DRESS SHOP
GENERAL JOURNAL   PAGE 9

Date		Account Titles and Description	PR		Dr.			Cr.	

MINI PRACTICE SET

THE CORNER DRESS SHOP
AUXILIARY PETTY CASH RECORD

Date	Voucher No.	Description	Receipts	Payment	Category of Payment					
					Postage Expense	Delivery Expense	Sundry			
							Account	Amount		

MINI PRACTICE SET

ACCOUNTS PAYABLE SUBSIDIARY LEDGER

NAME   BLEW CO. _____

Date 201X		Explanation	Post Ref.	Debit	Credit	Credit Balance
Mar	1	Balance	✔			1 9 0 0 00

NAME   JONES CO. _____

Date 201X		Explanation	Post Ref.	Debit	Credit	Credit Balance

NAME   MOE'S GARAGE _____

Date 201X		Explanation	Post Ref.	Debit	Credit	Credit Balance

MINI PRACTICE SET

NAME   MORRIS CO. _____

Date 201X		Explanation	Post Ref.	Debit	Credit	Credit Balance

ACCOUNTS RECEIVABLE SUBSIDIARY LEDGER

NAME   BING CO. _____

Date 201X		Explanation	Post Ref.	Debit	Credit	Debit Balance
Mar	1	Balance	✔			2 2 0 0 00

NAME   BLEW CO. _____

Date 201X		Explanation	Post Ref.	Debit	Credit	Debit Balance

MINI PRACTICE SET

NAME   RONALD CO. _____

Date 201X		Explanation	Post Ref.	Debit				Credit				Debit Balance			

GENERAL LEDGER

CASH   **ACCOUNT NO. 110**

Date 201X		Explanation	Post Ref.	Debit				Credit				Balance							
												Debit				Credit			
Mar	1	Balance	✔									2	2 3 1	90					

MINI PRACTICE SET

ACCOUNTS RECEIVABLE   ACCOUNT NO. 111

Date 201X		Explanation	Post Ref.	Debit	Credit	Balance Debit	Balance Credit
Mar	1	Balance	✔			2 2 0 0 00	

PETTY CASH   ACCOUNT NO. 112

Date 201X		Explanation	Post Ref.	Debit	Credit	Balance Debit	Balance Credit
Mar	1	Balance	✔			3 5 00	

MERCHANDISE INVENTORY   ACCOUNT NO. 114

Date 201X		Explanation	Post Ref.	Debit	Credit	Balance Debit	Balance Credit
Mar	1	Balance	✔			5 6 0 0 00	

MINI PRACTICE SET

PREPAID RENT   ACCOUNT NO. 116

Date 201X		Explanation	Post Ref.	Debit	Credit	Balance Debit	Balance Credit
Mar	1	Balance	✔			1 8 0 0 00	

DELIVERY TRUCK   ACCOUNT NO. 120

Date 201X		Explanation	Post Ref.	Debit	Credit	Balance Debit	Balance Credit
Mar	1	Balance	✔			6 0 0 0 00	

ACCUMULATED DEPRECIATION, TRUCK   ACCOUNT NO. 121

Date 201X		Explanation	Post Ref.	Debit	Credit	Balance Debit	Balance Credit
Mar	1	Balance	✔				1 5 0 0 00

MINI PRACTICE SET

ACCOUNTS PAYABLE   **ACCOUNT NO. 210**

Date 201X		Explanation	Post Ref.	Debit	Credit	Balance	
						Debit	Credit
Mar	1	Balance	✔				1 9 0 0 00

SALARIES PAYABLE   **ACCOUNT NO. 212**

Date 201X		Explanation	Post Ref.	Debit	Credit	Balance	
						Debit	Credit

FIT PAYABLE   **ACCOUNT NO. 214**

Date 201X		Explanation	Post Ref.	Debit	Credit	Balance	
						Debit	Credit
Mar	1	Balance	✔				1 0 1 3 00

MINI PRACTICE SET

FICA-OASDI PAYABLE   ACCOUNT NO. 216

Date 201X		Explanation	Post Ref.	Debit	Credit	Balance Debit	Balance Credit
Mar	1	Balance	✔				1 3 3 9 20

FICA-MEDICARE PAYABLE   ACCOUNT NO. 218

Date 201X		Explanation	Post Ref.	Debit	Credit	Balance Debit	Balance Credit
Mar	1	Balance	✔				3 1 3 20

SIT PAYABLE   ACCOUNT NO. 220

Date 201X		Explanation	Post Ref.	Debit	Credit	Balance Debit	Balance Credit
Mar	1	Balance	✔				7 5 6 00

SUTA TAX PAYABLE   ACCOUNT NO. 222

Date 201X		Explanation	Post Ref.	Debit	Credit	Balance Debit	Balance Credit
Mar	1	Balance	✔				9 7 9 20

FUTA TAX PAYABLE   ACCOUNT NO. 224

Date 201X		Explanation	Post Ref.	Debit	Credit	Balance Debit	Balance Credit
Mar	1	Balance	✔				1 6 3 20

UNEARNED RENT   ACCOUNT NO. 226

Date 201X		Explanation	Post Ref.	Debit	Credit	Balance Debit	Balance Credit
Mar	1	Balance	✔				8 0 0 00

MINI PRACTICE SET

B. LOEB, CAPITAL   ACCOUNT NO. 310

Date 201X		Explanation	Post Ref.	Debit	Credit	Balance Debit	Balance Credit
Mar	1	Balance	✔				9 1 0 3 10

B. LOEB, WITHDRAWALS   ACCOUNT NO. 320

Date 201X		Explanation	Post Ref.	Debit	Credit	Balance Debit	Balance Credit

INCOME SUMMARY   ACCOUNT NO. 330

Date 201X		Explanation	Post Ref.	Debit	Credit	Balance Debit	Balance Credit

SALES   ACCOUNT NO. 410

Date 201X		Explanation	Post Ref.	Debit	Credit	Balance Debit	Balance Credit

SALES RETURNS AND ALLOWANCES   ACCOUNT NO. 412

Date 201X		Explanation	Post Ref.	Debit	Credit	Balance Debit	Balance Credit

MINI PRACTICE SET

SALES DISCOUNT — ACCOUNT NO. 414

Date 201X	Explanation	Post Ref.	Debit	Credit	Balance Debit	Balance Credit

RENTAL INCOME — ACCOUNT NO. 416

Date 201X	Explanation	Post Ref.	Debit	Credit	Balance Debit	Balance Credit

PURCHASES — ACCOUNT NO. 510

Date 201X	Explanation	Post Ref.	Debit	Credit	Balance Debit	Balance Credit

PURCHASES RETURNS AND ALLOWANCES — ACCOUNT NO. 512

Date 201X	Explanation	Post Ref.	Debit	Credit	Balance Debit	Balance Credit

PURCHASES DISCOUNT — ACCOUNT NO. 514

Date 201X	Explanation	Post Ref.	Debit	Credit	Balance Debit	Balance Credit

MINI PRACTICE SET

SALES SALARY EXPENSE   ACCOUNT NO. 610

Date 201X		Explanation	Post Ref.	Debit	Credit	Balance	
						Debit	Credit

OFFICE SALARY EXPENSE   ACCOUNT NO. 611

Date 201X		Explanation	Post Ref.	Debit	Credit	Balance	
						Debit	Credit

PAYROLL TAX EXPENSE   ACCOUNT NO. 612

Date 201X		Explanation	Post Ref.	Debit	Credit	Balance	
						Debit	Credit

CLEANING EXPENSE   ACCOUNT NO. 614

Date 201X		Explanation	Post Ref.	Debit	Credit	Balance	
						Debit	Credit

DEPRECIATION EXPENSE, TRUCK   ACCOUNT NO. 616

Date 201X		Explanation	Post Ref.	Debit	Credit	Balance	
						Debit	Credit

MINI PRACTICE SET

RENT EXPENSE   ACCOUNT NO. 618

Date 201X	Explanation	Post Ref.	Debit	Credit	Balance Debit	Balance Credit

POSTAGE EXPENSE   ACCOUNT NO. 620

Date 201X	Explanation	Post Ref.	Debit	Credit	Balance Debit	Balance Credit

DELIVERY EXPENSE   ACCOUNT NO. 622

Date 201X	Explanation	Post Ref.	Debit	Credit	Balance Debit	Balance Credit

MISCELLANEOUS EXPENSE   ACCOUNT NO. 624

Date 201X	Explanation	Post Ref.	Debit	Credit	Balance Debit	Balance Credit

MINI PRACTICE SET

THE CORNER DRESS SHOP
SCHEDULE OF ACCOUNTS RECEIVABLE
MARCH 31, 201X

THE CORNER DRESS SHOP
SCHEDULE OF ACCOUNTS PAYABLE
MARCH 31, 201X

MINI PRACTICE SET

THE CORNER DRESS SHOP
INCOME STATEMENT
FOR MONTH ENDED MARCH 31, 201X

MINI PRACTICE SET

THE CORNER DRESS SHOP
STATEMENT OF OWNER'S EQUITY
FOR MONTH ENDED MARCH 31, 201X

MINI PRACTICE SET

THE CORNER DRESS SHOP
BALANCE SHEET
MARCH 31, 201X

MINI PRACTICE SET

THE CORNER DRESS SHOP
POST-CLOSING TRIAL BALANCE
MARCH 31, 201X

Name_____ Class_____ Date_____

MINI PRACTICE SET

Form **941 for 201X:** **Employer's QUARTERLY Federal Tax Return**   990106

(Rev. January 2006)   Department of the Treasury — Internal Revenue Service

                                                                          OMB No. 1545-0029

(EIN)
Employer identification number   ☐☐ – ☐☐☐☐☐☐☐

Name *(not your trade name)*

Trade name *(if any)*

Address
          Number   Street   Suite or room number

          City   State   ZIP code

Report for this Quarter ...
(Check one.)

☐ **1:** January, February, March

☐ **2:** April, May, June

☐ **3:** July, August, September

☐ **4:** October, November, December

Read the separate instructions before you fill out this form. Please type or print within the boxes.

Part 1: Answer these questions for this quarter.

1 Number of employees who received wages, tips, or other compensation for the pay period including: *Mar. 12* (Quarter 1), *June 12* (Quarter 2), *Sept. 12* (Quarter 3), *Dec. 12* (Quarter 4)   **1** ☐

2 Wages, tips, and other compensation . . . .   **2** ☐

3 Total income tax withheld from wages, tips, and other compensation . . . .   **3** ☐

4 If no wages, tips, and other compensation are subject to social security or Medicare tax . .   ☐ Check and go to line 6.

5 Taxable social security and Medicare wages and tips:

	Column 1		Column 2
5a Taxable social security wages	☐	× .124 =	☐
5b Taxable social security tips	☐	× .124 =	☐
5c Taxable Medicare wages & tips	☐	× .029 =	☐

5d Total social security and Medicare taxes (*Column 2*, lines 5a + 5b + 5c = line 5d) . .   **5d** ☐

6 Total taxes before adjustments (lines 3 + 5d = line 6) . . . .   **6** ☐

7 TAX ADJUSTMENTS (Read the instructions for line 7 before completing lines 7a through 7h.):

7a Current quarter's fractions of cents . . . .   ☐

7b Current quarter's sick pay . . . .   ☐

7c Current quarter's adjustments for tips and group-term life insurance   ☐

7d Current year's income tax withholding (attach Form 941c) . . .   ☐

7e Prior quarters' social security and Medicare taxes (attach Form 941c)   ☐

7f Special additions to federal income tax (attach Form 941c) . . .   ☐

7g Special additions to social security and Medicare (attach Form 941c)   ☐

7h TOTAL ADJUSTMENTS (Combine all amounts: lines 7a through 7g.)   **7h** ☐

8 Total taxes after adjustments (Combine lines 6 and 7h.) . . . .   **8** ☐

9 Advance earned income credit (EIC) payments made to employees . . . .   **9** ☐

10 Total taxes after adjustment for advance EIC (line 8 – line 9 = line 10) . . . .   **10** ☐

11 Total deposits for this quarter, including overpayment applied from a prior quarter . . .   **11** ☐

12 Balance due (If line 10 is more than line 11, write the difference here.) . . . .   **12** ☐
Make checks payable to *United States Treasury.*

13 Overpayment (If line 11 is more than line 10, write the difference here.)   ☐   Check one ☐ Apply to next return.
                                                                                    ☐ Send a refund.

▶ You **MUST** fill out both pages of this form and **SIGN** it.

Next ➡

For Privacy Act and Paperwork Reduction Act Notice, see the back of the Payment Voucher.   Cat. No. 17001Z   Form **941** (Rev. 1-2006)

MINI PRACTICE SET

990206

Name *(not your trade name)*	Employer identification number (EIN)

Part 2: Tell us about your deposit schedule and tax liability for this quarter.

If you are unsure about whether you are a monthly schedule depositor or a semiweekly schedule depositor, see *Pub. 15 (Circular E)*, section 11.

14 ☐ ☐ Write the state abbreviation for the state where you made your deposits OR write "MU" if you made your deposits in *multiple* states.

15 Check one: ☐ Line 10 is less than $2,500. Go to Part 3.

☐ You were a monthly schedule depositor for the entire quarter. Fill out your tax liability for each month. Then go to Part 3.

Tax liability: Month 1 ☐ ▪
Month 2 ☐ ▪
Month 3 ☐ ▪
Total liability for quarter ☐ ▪ Total must equal line 10.

☐ You were a semiweekly schedule depositor for any part of this quarter. Fill out *Schedule B (Form 941): Report of Tax Liability for Semiweekly Schedule Depositors*, and attach it to this form.

Part 3: Tell us about your business. If a question does NOT apply to your business, leave it blank.

16 If your business has closed or you stopped paying wages . . . . ☐ Check here, and

enter the final date you paid wages ☐ / /

17 If you are a seasonal employer and you do not have to file a return for every quarter of the year . . ☐ Check here.

Part 4: May we speak with your third-party designee?

Do you want to allow an employee, a paid tax preparer, or another person to discuss this return with the IRS? See the instructions for details.

☐ Yes. Designee's name _____

Phone ( ) – Personal Identification Number (PIN) ☐ ☐ ☐ ☐ ☐

☐ No.

Part 5: Sign here. You MUST fill out both sides of this form and SIGN it.

Under penalties of perjury, I declare that I have examined this return, including accompanying schedules and statements, and to the best of my knowledge and belief, it is true, correct, and complete.

✗ Sign your name here _____

Print name and title _____

Date ☐ / / Phone ( ) –

Part 6: For PAID preparers only *(optional)*

Paid Preparer's Signature	
Firm's name	
Address	EIN
	ZIP code
Date / / Phone ( ) –	SSN/PTIN
☐ Check if you are self-employed.	

Form **941** (Rev. 1-2006)